BEHINI

BEHIND MY SMILE

VINETTE HOFFMAN-JACKSON

An intimate story of one year in my life. A story of coercive control, domestic abuse, homelessness, unemployment, survival and triumph!
This is my story.

ISBN 978-1-912419-79-1

Printed and bound in Great Britain.
Published by YouCaxton Publications 2019
YCBN: 1.6

YouCaxton Publications

enquiries@youcaxton.co.uk

It is not what happens to you in life that matters.
It is how you respond to what happens,
that makes the difference.
~ Zig Ziglar

Acknowledgements

An attitude of gratitude keeps you humbled, balanced and grounded. It puts your life into unparalleled perspective. Regardless of your situation, as long as you are breathing, you have a reason and should always be grateful.

I am indeed grateful to and for so many people who have been a part of my life and my journey so far. To my family members who were my rock throughout a difficult year, I thank you. Special mention to my mother Teslyn Dawkins whom I adore and will forever honour and respect. I am privileged and grateful that you are my mother. To my sisters whose words of encouragement helped me to carry on one day at a time.

To Rodrigo, who entered my life at the darkest moment and like a roaring flame reignited my belief in love and life's dreams and led me out of my darkness.

To my three boys Matthew, Jonathan and Ethan. Your support, attitude and positive encouragement gives me calm reassurance that I have raised gentlemen who will no doubt leave this world a little bit better than they found it. I love you eternally.

My journey has taught me who my true friends are. When my mood inexplicably changed and I suddenly snapped at someone for no apparent reason or when I said I would do or go somewhere and didn't; my real friends, instead of getting upset or angry, reached out because they knew this was not the true me and realised something was wrong. To these friends I extend my heartfelt gratitude for not letting go even though I gave you enough reasons to.

And as always my sincerest appreciation and gratitude to the Pharaohs in my life. Without you this book would not have been possible. I would not have grown into a stronger and more determined woman. You have added the plots and twists to my story and fulfilled your role in my life. Thank you.

Contents

Introduction

I lost and gained so many people in my life in 2017, and undoubtedly many people may have changed their opinions of who they believed I was and what I represented because they did not know my struggles, nor could they comprehend that my smile was just a facade.

Throughout my journey I sometimes became unreasonable, unreliable and even unfriendly at times. There were times when I made plans with friends and, on my way, emotions would overtake me and I would find somewhere quiet and just cry for a while. I couldn't bring myself to call and speak to anyone or even offer an apology and so I just left it unexplained.

I would forget birthdays, anniversaries and important dates or I stopped calling to just say 'hi'. Friends who were struggling through illnesses could no longer count on my strength because I felt too weak myself. To these people I say, 'I am sorry'. I hope someday the people I have lost, may read and understand that, even though I was smiling, I was breaking inside and the pride in me meant I could not invite you to be a part of my journey. Sometimes a smile is so much more than just a smile; it hides more than it shows and that was certainly true in my case.

In 2016 I made a seemingly innocuous decision in my life that set me on a direct path to pain, loss and hurt. Just one decision taught me some of the greatest lessons in my life so far. Were it not for my faith, family and friends the ending might have been completely different.

Life is a learning process and it is in those moments

when you're feeling the most pain that you must harness all your inner strength and search to find the lessons being taught, find your message in the mess.

Quite often life's lessons are so painful that we focus all our energy on the pain instead of looking for the lesson. Initially this was true for me. I focussed on the hurt, the pain and the anger and briefly entertained thoughts of revenge but somehow, through the help of God, I managed to look beyond and managed to learn a lot in the process.

My faith was tested many times over and at times I wavered but every time I felt I was going to break, I prayed for some sign that God was still there and my signs always appeared. Matthew 7: vs 7 & 8: '*Ask, and it shall be given you; seek, and ye shall find; knock, and it shall be opened unto you. For every one that asketh receiveth; and he that seeketh findeth; and to him that knocketh it shall be opened.*'

This book is an outpouring of my heart. It was written in short bursts during the most painful time of my life. It was my healing, my catharsis and my reminder that I needed to carry on.

Behind this smile

You ask me why I smile
Am I happy or feeling fine?
You look at me with puzzled eyes
Searching my face for any give-away signs.
You may have sensed there was something wrong
That my smile somehow does not belong.

I smile because it is simply what I choose to do
I smile to stop myself from crying
To stop myself from slowly dying
I smile to hold back these tears
And mask these hidden fears

I smile because. . .
It gives me healing
stops me from feeling
hides the bruising
And eases the pain.

You ask me why I smile
I smile to stem the flow of my broken emotions
It anchors me as I am tossed amongst tumultuous waves,
seeking peace.

This smile
keeps me sane.

Chapter 1
Your lights are still on!

I am Lost

I closed my eye
As if to die
To avoid the sounds so loud
And escape this maddening crowd.
I pretended I was dead
To get the noises from my head
I turned inwards and ran away
To make sure I survived another day.
I ran and ran inside my mind
Until a way out I could not find
In panic I screamed aloud
But no whimper from the now silent crowd
And the tears started to freely flow
Because I did not know where I should go.
Too late, I realise the full cost
I'm in my mind and I am lost!

Today, after I dropped my three boys off at school, I suddenly felt close to tears. My heart raced, my headed pounded and my breathing became shallow and raspy. Before I could think rationally, tears stung my eyes and I quickly and rapidly batted my eyelids in short succession to ease the stinging and stem the flow of my tears. I used the back of my right hands to wipe away the few errant tears that had escaped before I had time to think.

I needed a break, I thought to myself. Some time to switch off, recharge and try to live again. I whispered a quick petition to God, hoping this time he would answer.

Absentmindedly, I reached for my phone from my bag on the front passenger seat then rang my job. I was grateful no one answered, so I quickly left a voicemail and a very vague excuse. I told them I was not coming in because something had gone wrong at home; it was not a lie.

Instead of driving to work that morning and following my normal pattern, and without any pre-planning, I found myself slowly driving in the direction of an isolated park nearby that I had passed on a number of previous occasions. It was just a few miles away. I drove so slowly that the busy rush-hour traffic piled up behind me and somewhere in the quiet dark recesses of my mind I thought I could hear the angry horns of cars bleating, interrupted only by the occasional swear words. I could sense flashing lights but I blocked them all out. I was in a zombie-like trance and completely oblivious to my surroundings. The radio was off but there was a song in my head and I hummed the tune, no words, just a dull, haunting, quiet melody. It seemed to calm me and dull the aching pain I felt in my heart. My opened eyes focussed on nothing in particular and saw no one in particular, just the open road and I drove only from past memory.

Eventually and miraculously, I got to the park and started

to drive even slower than I was driving before, looking around to find the most secluded, isolated spot possible. My song was still playing loudly in my head and I hummed even louder and even started rocking my head from side to side in time with the imaginary beat. The melody or rhythm did not follow any pattern or particular tune, it was just a soothing melody that I had created in my head. I was locked away in my own world and, for that moment, I could see nothing and no one, could sense nothing and feel nothing. I was numb. Nothing mattered.

I drove around for a few minutes, searching for the perfect spot. After a while I found a quiet, isolated spot where I was highly unlikely to be disturbed by anyone for a while. I drove towards a great big tree with bare branches reaching out in all directions like old witches' fingers trying to catch anything that came within its grasp. I smiled, my first reaction to anything external since I left my boys at school. I drove slowly into their waiting embrace and stopped about three inches from the base of the tree. I turned my head to look through my rear-view window just to make sure no one was watching or near enough to see or hear me. The park was completely deserted and I felt relieved. I turned the car engine off and adjusted my seat into a semi-reclining position so I was not visible to any unwelcome eyes that might choose to wander by. Satisfied that I was completely hidden, I gently closed my eyes and put my right arm across my eyes to block out any light and just lay there.

Thinking nothing, doing nothing, just being in the

moment, listening to all the sounds and trying to figure out their source and their positions relative to each other, I could hear rustling as the leaves swayed in the gentle wind through my slightly opened roof window and the distant hum of the traffic. A dog barked somewhere; it sounded happy and I was momentarily jealous of the freedom the dog had. I listened for a few seconds then its continuous happy barking became slightly irritating. The dog had no worries and no care and I tried my best to block out that tiny bit of joy. I put my fingers in my ears and once again started humming my tune.

I wanted to be in complete physical darkness, I was already there mentally and emotionally. I did not want to hear or see or even feel anything. I wanted to just disappear. My life at that moment felt like I was in pitch black darkness with no lights anywhere, not even a candle that I could reach for to give me some type of hope. All that I could see or think about was enveloped in darkness. It was Friedrich Nietzsche who once said 'If you stare into the abyss, the abyss stares back at you' and so I could feel the darkness creeping into me. I stayed in the darkness for a while, basking in its stillness and the unsettling peace it brought. I could feel myself going deeper into the silence and somewhere in my subconscious somehow I knew if I kept going, I might never return.

Sometimes in life, if we are not careful, problems and circumstances can overwhelm us and blot our all the little light sources that are still there.

I desperately started searching for my light sources. I

thought of God and thanked him that I was still alive. I thought of my children and some silly things they had done and a *genuine* smile formed on my lips. I thought of my mom and grandmother and immediately I felt my shoulders straighten because they had instilled in me a strength that I could feel each time I thought about them, There was still some light in my life.

I allowed myself a few moments to focus on some positives in my life before I slowly allowed my mind to drift back to the last few months of my life, and the pain and heartache that the memories brought with it.

I journeyed back to where I believed all my problems started, with one simple innocent decision. It is difficult to believe, but every decision, every choice, every action has the potential to change your life forever and redirect it along a path you never dreamed of before. I was angry with myself about this one single, seemingly innocuous decision that had changed my life so radically and immersed me in this pit of despair. It was hard to believe, but it had and I struggled with the repercussions. I felt trapped and all alone.

I was never a big sharer of my personal life and so everything was kept bottled up inside me which heightened all my emotions and reactions a million times over. I learned later that in time of trouble, it is a mistake to build walls like a dam to contain your emotions because when the storm starts to rage, if that dam wall breaks then you will wash away not only the thorns in your life but the roses will also be battered and destroyed. It is important to find a run off, some outlet to reduce the pressure so even in the storms, there will still be a certain calm and your emotions will be controlled.

It may be impossible to believe, but just thinking about my life made me feel physical pain. As I started to feel the pressure in my chest building, it was as if someone was sitting on me and I struggled to breathe. I could feel a heaviness in my eyes and a huge lump forming in my throat, then I felt it, a cool trail left by a single tear that gently rolled down my left cheek. Then a second one followed, then both eyes glazed over with rivulets of tears, following the contours of my face and dripping from my chin. More teardrops kept coming, steadily increasing their frequency, with a few lingering at the corners of my lips. I could taste their saltiness as I licked my dry lips unconsciously. The trickle quickly became a torrent until eventually it became a deluge punctuated by an occasional loud, audible sob, little whimpers at first then great big ones that shook my entire body. I felt my chest tighten and I hugged myself and closed my eyes tightly to ebb the flow but the tears still fought their way through at the corners of my eyes. The dam had broken and there was no other outlet.

I opened my eyes, blinking rapidly. For the first time in a long while I did not hold back. I cried. I cried as a child cries, with no thoughts about how I sounded, how I looked or who would see. I cried aloud. I cried to God. I cried to the Universe. I cried to anyone or anything that would listen. I cried.

Then the questions started in my mind but they too needed an outlet so I became verbal and so I screamed out aloud into thin air, hopeful they would reach someone or something that could offer an answer.

'Why?'

'Why me?'

'What have I ever done?'

'Why can't I get a break?'

I didn't ask politely, I screamed each question aloud, punctuated and separated only by tears and loud screams that tore at the silence and drowned out all the other sounds. I was seated upright now and I pounded the steering wheel because the tears and screams could not provide enough of an outlet for these pent-up emotions that were long denied any avenue to escape. They were valid questions and I wanted answers and I wanted them now. I screamed because I wanted my questions at the front of the queue because at that moment I felt they were the most important questions in the universe and I deserved to get my answers.

I justified my questions by reminding the universe that I was a good person and I did not deserve this; I deserved good things. I listed my attributes aloud: I was kind, I was helpful, I believed in God. I deserved good things, I screamed.

After what felt like an eternity, the tears subsided, my throat was dry and still no answer came. I felt disappointed and abandoned. It was as if I had expected some type of epiphany or miraculous intervention that would immediately remedy my situation. I felt as if I was somehow going to drive out of that park with every detail of my life sorted or at least a plan in my head to tell me exactly what I should do next. In that moment I wholeheartedly believed I would get some type of answer.

When you have no more care or feel numb and empty, you develop a certain feeling that nothing is impossible and miracles will happen. Your desperation eliminates all physical barriers and you somehow feel everything can change in an instant. You somehow expect to be closer to the creator and feel something or get some sign to show he was listening, and I was at that point in my life but sadly no answer came.

When the tears had completely stopped and my voice was just a raspy whisper, I gently leaned back once again into my reclining seat and stared. I did not focus on anything in particular; I just stared and saw nothing. I could still feel the ever present and painful lump in my throat each time I attempted to swallow. I just lay there and waited, staring blankly at the roof of my car, waiting, waiting for nothing in particular but expecting something, anything. I waited for any slight sign that my cries were heard and were being attended to. I waited in silence as the vacuum created by my screams slowly cracked and the sounds of the park slowly trickled back into my consciousness. Still I listened and waited, resolute that I would get some answer that day.

The brutal realisation slowly dawned on me - no help was coming today - and the darkness once again slowly enveloped my mind, my heart and my soul. I was lost and alone. I shivered as if a cold wind had blown into my car and my body responded by making myself smaller and wrapping my hand around my torso. I turned my head to the windows to check if I had opened them but they were still up.

My situation and circumstances had not changed in the few minutes, I had been locked in my car, crying gently. I closed my eyes once more with an accepted resignation to my desperate situation and drifted off to sleep.

*****

I was away in the land of dreams and some temporary relief from my life when I was suddenly jolted back to reality by a sharp rap on my driver's window. I sat up quickly, half frightened and half awake. I quickly wiped my eyes for them to get accustomed to the sudden lit environment and without any rational thought I attempted to straighten my weave and rubbed my hand over my eyes twice. Satisfied that I was more presentable to the world, I turned. 'Yes,' I mouthed though the closed window.

I could see his mouth moving but could not hear what he was saying. I glanced around and could see no one else in the park except a little shaggy brown dog prancing about a few feet away barking happily. I assumed they were together. I knitted my brows together to form a scowl. It must have been the happy dog I had heard earlier. I quickly glanced at the man standing by my window. He looked about seventy unless he had had a very hard life. He had kind wrinkles and had on a brown hat with red stripes that looked as if it had been worn through many winters. His coat was almost threadbare and I was not sure if brown was the original colour or age had caused all the colour to merge into one. One hand remained firmly in his pocket and the other held a chew toy, confirming that the shaggy brown dog was his. From all appearances he was just an old man out walking his dog but you couldn't miss his kind eyes and the warm smile that lingered at the corners of his lips. I slowly opened my window slightly to about a few inches. One still had to be careful.

The old man pointed towards the front of my car, 'Sorry ma'am' he said ' your light is still on!'

' Oh, thank you,' I muttered gratefully and even managed a half smile too.

He hesitated for about two seconds tilted his head then walked away calling to the brown shaggy dog. He had not commented on anything else even though my cheeks were stained with tear marks and I was a woman alone, dressed for work and sleeping in the park. I was grateful he had not asked before he walked away.

It would be months later when I reflected on this incident that I would realise that the old man gave me the answer I was waiting on, indirectly. He told me that my lights were still on, he reminded me that I was still alive. Even though I felt like my life was over, the fact that I was still breathing meant I was still alive and as long as you are alive there is hope. Hope that life will get better, hope that things will change, hope for a better day.

I switched off the car lights and glanced at the clock. . It was now 10 am and I had been in the park for over two hours. I briefly entertained the thought of going to work but one look at my face in the mirror told me this was not a great idea. There was no sense going to work in this state and I certainly did not want to go home, although it was not really a home. It was just a house. A house with thirty-two doors which might seem like an irrelevant fact but I had spent time counting every single one. I suppose it was just the same irrelevant mundane task that prisoners do to break the monotony and pass the time. I counted the doors because it felt like my prison. I longed to escape and break free but I realised that sometimes physical bars are much easier to break than emotional and mental bars. I was trapped and scarily no one on the outside knew.

*****

I lowered myself back into a semi-reclined position again and went back to staring at nothing in particular for a few minutes, then my stomach rumbled to remind me I still had not eaten any breakfast. I squeezed my tummy muscles to silence the rumble as I did not have the energy or inclination to move; I just wanted to sit and stare and be. My stomach however would not be silenced and started to grumble even louder this time. I decided I would drive to mask the sounds of my stomach and distract myself from the craving for a hot cup of cappuccino. I decided to drive around and until it was time to collect my eldest son (Son 1) and go to the house. I was in no mood to eat. Well at least that was a positive as I might even lose a few pounds, I smiled.

I turned on my radio and changed the station until I

found some soothing music. I switched on my engine to check my petrol gauge. I had enough petrol and nowhere in particular to go but I put the gear in drive and pressed the accelerator. The cry had given me a little more lucidity and I felt a bit lighter and was in the moment. I decided I would just drive to add further clarity to my troubled mind.

One of the greatest secrets or beauties of England is the numerous quiet lanes and lonely country roads that one can take to quiet the mind and fill the soul. I loved that. I drove and sang each song that came on the radio on the top of my voice and when I didn't know the words I made them up. I felt free as I was living in the moment and my mind was not focussed on the past or the future, only the now.

I spent the rest of the morning driving, stopping only for quick a bathroom break at random coffee shops and supermarkets. I did not want to be in the company of people that day; I just wanted my thinking space and nature. At about half past one I lost the battle with my stomach and went in search of food. There were no visible signs of commerce so I pulled over to check my glove compartment and luckily found a few cereal bars that I had left there for such emergencies. Well this was just such an occasion. I ate all three bars and drank a half-finished bottle of water I found on my back seat, no thought of Legionnaires' Disease.

Brunch finished, I started driving again, singing loudly. I had decided in my mind that the world could wait for today. I was just one person anyway so I wouldn't be missed from the bigger picture.

I drove to keep my sanity and in search of some inner peace. It was therapeutic.

Miles later, a sign with a clock at the bottom caught my eye and jolted me back to reality. I suddenly realised that Ii was almost fifty miles away from where I should be. I realised it would be impossible to get back to Luton on time to collect my eldest son, I had to arrange collection or another mode of transportation for him.

I found a junction and a tiny area where I could pull over and texted him to ask if he had cash with him. When he texted back in the affirmative I told him to take the train home this evening. I would meet him at the train station. I knew he would become anxious about going home alone. He suffered from Asperger's and he was also struggling with the existing situation. He had also counted all the doors.

Life can sometimes be difficult for many of us but somehow we manage to hold it together despite the odds being against us. It is in these moments that greatness is cultivated, when you triumph against all odds and make it through. I have always been a strong-minded and strong-willed person, like a bamboo that bends instead of breaking during the storms of life. Life however becomes extremely difficult when you're not only fighting for yourself but you are fighting for others. In my case I was also fighting for my children which made my life even more difficult each day. But the task of fighting for them somehow gave me more inner strength than I ever thought I had.

I quickly programmed my GPS and the expected time of arrival meant I could still collect my other two sons from school. They would be delighted to see me. Suddenly a wave of anxiety and borderline fear permeated my entire body and I shuddered involuntarily. I paused for a moment, my finger poised over my phone, and I could feel my heartbeat quicken. I took a few deep, slow breaths for a few seconds and when my heartbeat had slowed down to an acceptable pace, I started texting 'him'.

Who exactly was 'him'? '*Him*' was my self-appointed prison warden. Even the mere mention of his name to this very day causes me to feel as if I was drifting on a sea of hopelessness and pain. I chose to text as it meant I did not have to hear his voice.

For now, I will call him Mr X, but there are so many more things I could call him. I informed Mr X that I would collect my other two boys from school. He would normally do this part of the school run on some days but my sons hated it. My heart started beating rapidly and my breathing became shallow as I waited anxiously for his reply.

He immediately wanted to know why - which was what I expected and dreaded. Time to make up a quick lie, I thought. I texted then deleted then texted and deleted, just to make sure I got all the words right. My response could have far-reaching consequences which would not only impact on me but on my children. I had to protect them at all cost because that is just what mothers do.

I texted back and lied that my afternoon meeting was cancelled today and I wanted to rush home. Maybe that was a bit too dry I thought, and I quickly followed with a second text to tell him how much I loved him'. Just texting the words felt repulsive but for now, I had to. He did not respond and I preferred the silence.

It was early 2017.

Chapter 2
Bread ends and breasts!

Bread ends and breasts
I bet you'll never guess the rest
Never the two have been in the same space
But just in case
You start to wonder
and stress and ponder
I'll put you out of your misery
By sharing a childhood memory.

In mid December 2016 I found out that writing my thoughts and emotions down brought me some welcome distraction from life as I knew it and so I started writing random things down. Sometimes my thoughts came in the form of poetry, at times short reflective stories or sometimes just a narrative. I embraced the process and wrote. It was my escape, to prevent pressure building up behind the dam of emotions in my head. Speaking was also an escape avenue. It helped me to cope as I was able to release a little of my pent-up emotions and it stopped me from crying on a daily basis.

Whenever I gave a speech people would tell me how connected they felt to my speech. I would always respond by telling them that it was because my speeches came from my heart, they were not made-up stories. I always spoke with a smile so I doubt they believed me but that was okay.

I preferred my life like that: compartmentalised, let the world see the facade while I keep the hurt and pain hidden from view, visible only through my writings or speeches.

Although I tried never to share too much of my personal story, I secretly hoped someone could one day see beyond the smile and rescue me. Maybe someday.

At this point let me digress to give you some context and background of my life so that you will understand my story a bit better.

*****

Let me take you briefly back to my childhood in Jamaica. I grew up in a tiny fishing village called Barking Lodge on the eastern end of the island. I had an amazing childhood with many fond memories that are still shared between myself and my siblings. I was the only child between my parents and the eldest for my mother. We were not rich but it never really mattered. I grew up in an extended family with mother, father, grandmother, grandfather, uncles, aunts and cousins all within five miles of each other. I was brought up in the true sense of the phrase 'raised by a village'.

As a child I remember being constantly scolded for laughing too much. My grandmother would constantly threaten me by saying, 'If I ever see your teeth one more time you see.' Instead of laughing out loud I would then snicker, keeping my lips closed. She was right in scolding me because I would literally laugh at any and everything. I remember one Sunday Old Miss Nancy was stopping by for a visit when she slipped in the mud and fell over, sending one shoe flying and her glasses perched precariously on the bridge of her nose. Everyone who saw rushed out to help … all except me. I couldn't contain myself; I was laughing and rolling on the floor until two slaps from my grandmother knocked the humour right out of me. When a visiting minister was chased by a dog I had to sleep by my uncle's house to escape my grandmother's wrath. Although, in hindsight, I was more scared of God's punishment for laughing at his servant than of my grandmother than night.

It was just my nature to laugh first. I even laughed at myself when I tripped and spilled my entire dinner one Sunday afternoon. Although I cannot remember too clearly I am sure my grandmother laughed at me then. I am glad I learned to laugh early as it has been a quality that has helped me to cope. Laughing is medicine for the soul.

I have so many many memories but there is one I would love to share with you now. It is a memory that has come back to me during this time. Although it was long-forgotten and buried, it came back to me recently and I realised that some adults are just big children with responsibilities. It provides a bit of background to my current story. As the time is long past, the conversations, as most of the conversations in this book, are from my memory and so forgotten blanks I tried to fill in as best as possible to enable my story to flow.

*****

As I said before, I grew up with one brother, two sisters and numerous cousins and extended family members, and I have the fondest memories of our escapades and the trouble we caused or got into. We could not afford elaborate luxurious items, but simple things like a new shoe or a dress that was not made by a dressmaker or a local shoemaker was priceless. . We were poor but had so much fun and exciting times growing up together that money was irrelevant to us as children.

When I was about eleven and a half, I suddenly became aware that I was developmentally challenged. Not through any deep introspection or accidental self-discovery but from a very public declaration in the changing room from an 'over-developed' peer of mine.

'Oh my gosh! ' she declared in a voice as if she had discovered the answer to the biggest conspiracy theory in history and wanted her moment of fame as the one who solved it. Her sudden exclamation resulted in the entire group of about twelve girls in various state of undress looking around at the cause of such an audacious burst of excitement. They did not need to search very long to find the cause of her outburst as the girl at the centre of the conspiracy solution, a skinny twelve-year-old in advanced puberty, extended her index finger in my direction, and although she was at least ten feet away, it seemed to touch my very soul and left a chill and it felt like my blood and my entire body was frozen and I could not move.

'She has no breasts!' she screeched like an old witch and her shoulders shook as the raucous laughter escaped her lips causing her body to heave in convulsions as she struggled and failed to catch each breath. Each girl looked from my accuser and her somewhat animated movements to my flat chest on display because I had forgotten to cover up and I stood frozen in my tracks. There were a few hushed giggles and two or three of the girls laughed loudly too but most of the other girls thankfully just looked on with complete indifference and nonchalance.

I looked around at the mixture of expressions through misty curtains as the tears welled up in my eyes. The changing room suddenly felt way too small, extremely hot and very cramped.

My best friend who stood next to me suddenly shouted. ' Shut up Meg!!' she screamed at the top of her lungs in her haste to defend me and diverted all the attention to herself. In that split second, I unfroze and quickly grabbed my shirt, tugging and pulling at the fabric in a desperate bid to cover my chest quickly.

The sudden outburst from my best friend caused Meg to increase the volume of her raucous laughter. Her high-pitched shrieks alerted the boys next door who were also mid-way through the process of changing into their PE gears. They all rushed to the door of the girls' changing room to investigate the source of the laughter. 'What's going on in there?' they enquired. 'Who's laughing? Come one share the joke,' they continued as they desperately tried to peek around the corner. No one spoke or even attempted an answer. We were at the age when boys were only just tolerated but no one cared about them. They were just so annoying and loud. All the girls could agree on that fact so whether we were enemies or friends we were all united against boys.

We completely ignored their questions and a few girls

even went to make sure that the doors were securely locked then returned to continue changing. The boys eventually wandered off after being ignored.

The commotion caused by the boys proved to be a welcomed distraction. A few of the girls looked at me after the boys had left and immediately became disinterested and went back to their own conversations. Grateful for the now depleting attention I slowly turned and went back to changing for the physical education class, albeit a bit more self-consciously.

The day's activities went at their usual brisk pace and the incident in the changing room was just as quickly forgotten and disappeared to the recesses of my classmates' minds, but not mine. It lingered and lingered and planted the feeling of being slightly less endowed than the other girls in my year group. I felt like an outcast and I felt different. My friends tried their best to reassure me that I was okay and Meg was just out to cause some trouble that day. 'It will be someone else tomorrow, just watch,' Juliet said. I nodded and smiled but my smile did not come from the heart; my lips just curled to give the outward appearance but inside I was crying. Over time I would eventually master the art of smiling from the lips to disguise any pain that my heart felt.

Days passed then months, and my focus became more intensive about my flat chest. Nothing was happening and I was desperate to embrace puberty. One day I became brave enough and I spoke to my mom about it. She would always give the same answer: 'Don't worry, you're just a late bloomer,' she explained. But exactly how late would it be? I didn't want to ask any more questions so I let the issue drop. I also did not want my nosy cousins to overhear anything I was saying.

Mom just did not understand. I wanted to be like everyone else and fit in right now not later. My concerns were justified because as soon as I exited the kitchen where I was talking to my mother, I bumped into my older male cousin. He had the biggest grin on his face indicating that he had clearly overheard everything that was said. I squinted and furrowed my brows and yelled at him to go away. My cousin however found it hilarious and from that point he mercilessly teased me. I was call 'flat chest', 'boy in girls body' and countless other names. In those days teasing was brutal. You had to pretend it didn't bother you one bit and even learn to laugh along even though the joke was on you. It was the only protection against a nickname sticking to you for life. The reverse psychology of laughing it off meant your tormentor would soon lose interest as his efforts were not causing sufficient distress.

I laughed at first but he was persistent and relentless with his teasing. I spent many days crying or screaming at him. I hated him then and his lack of understanding for the most important period in a girl's life, her teenage years.

His cruelty and teasing came in many different forms and they seemed to get a bit cleverer and sophisticated each time as if hours of thought had been poured into their execution. One morning he walked into the room where I was sitting wearing an old bra stuffed with tissues and quickly broadcast it to all the children in our age-range. My other cousins found it hilarious but I did not. On another occasion at dinner he loudly declared to my mother, 'Can I please have the leg, Vinette prefers the breast!' as he reached for a piece of chicken. I reacted without thought and threw a spoon at him. I was promptly reprimanded by my mom and grandmother like a double tag team and sent outside.

'B-b-but... ' I attempted to explain but words failed me. What exactly could I say? So instead, I left it. 'Sorry' I mumbled to mom but I could feel the tears welling up inside my eyes. I ended up sweeping the entire yard as punishment. My cousin showed no remorse, clutching his arm where the spoon had just gently grazed him and twisting his face as if he had been wounded in some great war. There were no smiles from me, just plain anger.

A few days and with no more teasing from my cousin I assumed the episode had passed and he was now targeting someone else. I was wrong; it was just the calm before the storm. He had decided to up his game and go for the home run and I did not see it coming.

His final attempt at humiliating me affected me the most and it is the one I will always remember - the 'bread end ' fiasco. It has stood the memory test of time because it was so sinister and it elevated his teasing to actual cold-hearted, calculating, trouble-making, blame-taking terror.

It was a Saturday and that meant shopping at the local market. Mom had just returned with freshly baked bread so you could smell it from all the rooms in the house. It was a little bit of heaven especially when growing up poor.

My cousin approached me shortly after mom came home and apologised for being such a pain over the past few weeks. He explained that he was just messing about and having fun but he saw the impact his teasing had on me and he was truly sorry. He even managed to well up with tears. Sensing some sincerity I accepted his apology.

He turned to walk away then stopped with his back still turned, paused for about five seconds then started walking again. Puzzled, I asked 'are you okay?' He stopped again, turned and walked back towards where I was standing. He lowered his voice and told me he had heard something and although he was not sure it would work he encouraged me to try it and see if it would speed up my development. Naturally I was immediately curious but sensibly I was a bit cautious and so I acted very restrained. I showed no eagerness or at least pretended not to.

Sensing a lack of interest, he shrugged his shoulders and said, ' well, if you're not interested then…' and turned to walk away. He took a few steps as I stood there willing him to turn around but he didn't, he just kept on walking.

When he was almost at the corner of the house and would disappear from my line of sight I shouted, 'well tell me then, what is it? '

He hesitated a moment before turning around heaving a heavy sigh as if he had already forgotten our conversation and was already busy thinking about something else. In about five giant steps he was next to me. With a slight irritation in his voice and a quick check to see if anyone else was there he placed his arms around my shoulders. I shifted uncomfortably. I knitted my brow and squinted my eyes. Trust was not a thing easily repaired.

He guided me slowly away from the house towards a fruit tree in our back yard, delaying the moment with such practiced precision to get the most from the moment. He lowered his tone once again like a spy about to spill some secret that only he knew and knew that the person was desperate to hear. 'Right, listen I am not saying it is going to work. I have no proof. I am just sharing what I heard.' He paused for me to acknowledge and give my imaginary signature to his indemnity waiver claims. I nodded. 'Ok,' he continued satisfied with the nod. 'I hear' he once again glanced around then leaned into me, shifting so he was in front of me with both hands holding my shoulders he looked into my eyes 'if you eat the ends of a freshly baked bread slowly, chewing each bite twenty-five times it produces some type of body chemical that will take care of your flat chest.' My mouth fell open. I was not sure if it was in disbelief or the knowledge of such a simple solution to my problem. He sensed a bit of hesitation and quickly added, ' don't you see Miss Sue from down the fish stall? Well which part of bread you always see her eating?'

It was true. Ms Sue was very well endowed and always showed a preference for the crust of the bread, the bread-ends. My mouth opened wider and I realise its increasing circumference only by a sharp pain at the corners of my mouth. I slammed my mouth shut so quickly it made a sound. The loss of circumference in my mouth was immediately transferred to my eyes until they also hurt from lack of blinking. I stood paralysed.

My cousin skulked away without even a backward glance. I just stood there for what seemed like an eternity. By my mental calculation I needed about a hundred loaves of bread but I needed to start today. PE was next Monday and I had bunked and hidden away from the changing room for months now. This could be the comeback I wanted bread-end breasts!

As if on cue that smell of bread came back to tantalise my nostrils but this time the odour had a new found charm and I could already feel my breasts growing. I quickly ran inside. Mom was grating coconuts while seated on a tree stump in the yard and my grandad was sitting on a log shooting the breeze with my cousins, including my saviour. He caught my eye and winked. He knew the task I was about to undertake; it was our secret.

I backed my way into the house and saw the freshly baked loaf of bread just laying there on the dining table. Some of the middle slices had already been eaten but it didn't matter because the bread ends were still there. Growing up we had to ask for food so I was glad it was not a new unopened bag, I cautiously and quietly opened the tied bag and took the two bread-ends out then returned the bread to the table, trying to put it in the exact position I found it. I would not waste time asking permission to take two slices of bread, just in case I got a no.

I snuck outside towards the front of the house to avoid the adults in the backyard. I sat under my favourite tree and starting eating my bread-ends, chewing at speed and mentally counting to twenty five, both because I wanted quick results and the thought that I did not want to get caught. I was well into the second bread piece when there was a loud clatter and I swivelled my head to see my mom, arms akimbo standing in the middle of scattered pots and pans which had obviously fallen or dropped from her hands. The huge din caused me to almost choke. I gulped hard and swallowed the now bitter-tasting bread in my mouth. Instinctively my hand holding the remaining uneaten bread-end slowly slid behind my back and a silly misplaced grin covered my lips. ‘ M-m-m-mom, you alright?’ I almost whispered, a squeaky voice betraying the fear I felt and my racing heart. Although I already knew she was not.

‘Vinette Fay Marcia Hoffman who give you bread to eat?” The full name, ouch! The full name was always a dead giveaway that she was angry. I always wondered why parents would recite the full names when you got into trouble and years later I was able to make very valid connections to why this happened. As a child the only other times the full name was used was during a funeral or during a wedding and as both religious practices signified the end of something, I assumed the full name meant it was the end of you. I started to cry. ‘Don't badda cry, save your strength,’ my mother commanded and took two steps towards me.

You did not need to be an A* student to recognise that you had only one option in these types of scenario. Run! I quickly assessed her speed, the look on her face and made the quick decision to drop the piece of bread and run for my just dear life. I was lither and quicker but she had bigger steps; just as her finger tips reached out to grab me I bent low which would have been a priceless move in a slow motion flick. Her hands grazed the top of my head and she was off balance for a millisecond which was just enough time for me to dart around the corner of the house and head for freedom. Freedom meant reaching that mango tree before my mother. She was still in hot pursuit but I got to the base of the tree first and without even a pause I was climbing that tree like a master. When I was safely at the top I sat on the top limb and started breathing heavily. My mom stood at the bottom of the tree pacing. ' Ok, sleep up there tonight!' she instructed.

I was just about to offer my plea and give my explanation when my peripheral vision caught sight of my cousin on the other side of the house. He was rolling on the grass laughing his head off. Holding on to his sides in hysterics. He was however careful not to make a racket and so all you could see was the little snake writhing around and thinly muffled snickers escaping from his mouth. At that moment it all became clear. My cousin had once again managed to get me into trouble and escaped scot-free.

What could you say when you are the one caught eating the bread and how could you even attempt to explain the reason behind the misdemeanour. So instead I remained silent and sat on my branch waiting for nightfall when hopefully everyone would have forgotten and when my uncle came back from work.

*****

My cousin was always the one to create mischief when I was growing up. He would orchestrate things from behind the scenes but somehow he was clever enough to never get caught. He could anticipate every move before it happened and side-step it in a bid to escape any blame or consequences. It always frustrated me and even though I complained and cried, no one seemed to believe me. The circumstances and evidence just did not support my side of events.

Years after I had grown up I thought I had escaped this childhood nightmare but in 2016 I was once again a victim of a well-orchestrated and elaborate plan to destabilise, humiliate and take my parental rights away for my youngest son. Only this time, I decided I would not sit quietly and wait for nightfall when all would be forgotten. This time I would be bold and tell my story.

Chapter 3
Mr X

In May 2016, an old flame, well to be honest, not a flame but an old flicker re-entered my life. He was the father of my last son. We had always had an unspoken arrangement where we were in firm agreement that we passionately disliked (*I am being kind*) each other and somehow we managed to accept that as a permanent pervading feeling that would never change.

However, occasionally we looked past our hatred or dislike for each other and tried to be civil for some common cause, usually Son 3. It was a very rare occurrence and I was okay with the arrangement. His sister disliked me and I disliked her. His brother in law tolerated me and I tolerated him. His mother unfortunately was dead. My mother unfortunately wished *he* was dead.

After a few texts here and there earlier in the year, I decided for the sake of our son to meet up on a platonic basis at first , which we did several times over the next few months.

After years of unpaid child support and lack of parental engagement he suddenly decided he wanted to be a *better* man, well at least a man, and I was okay with that. He started helping out financially and I was grateful for the assistance. To be honest I felt it was owed to me after years of non-payment and little or no help whatsoever. It seemed he had finally turned over a new leaf and I relaxed a bit although wary because he had previously done the Mr

Nice guy routine and then disappeared. Little did I know at the time that this was an elaborate plan to destabilise and humiliate me and an attempt to take my child away from me. The same child he had walked away from because I had refused the termination he requested, the same child that he had refuse to acknowledge or sign the birth certificate for, the same child whom I would have to drive miles just to establish some paternal family contact.

In June, after a few meetings without any incidents, he brazenly asked if he could move in with me and I brazenly said 'No!' I was so proud of myself. Mr Nice guy or Mr Bad guy, whatever his persona was this time, I was not going to be pulled into cohabiting with this person ever again. The world believed the devil wore Prada but I knew different. I knew what he wore and how he smelled. He accepted my decision and so we continued the occasional visitations at random places so he could bond with his child. We would meet at cafés, parks or his sister's home to facilitate father-and-son time.

He would occasionally visit me and tried to play daddy to my three sons but the two older boys would just do the polite 'hello' and rush off; they could smell the devil too and they did not like it. Children somehow are better judges of character than adults; they can sense things before we do, but as adults we sometimes ignore their intuitions and I suspect over time they eventually lose that and become us.

I did not try to convince the boys to do anything or act in anyway that they would feel uncomfortable. They had to be true to who they were and I respected their feelings. As a mother I wanted them to be free to express themselves as long as they were polite and not disrespectful to anyone.

His visits continued and, to be honest, his financial help was welcome. I was a single mother to three boys. But life never flows smoothly for long and, as if on cue, my landlady called me in summer 2016 to explain that she had sold the house and had to give me notice. It came at the most inopportune time but I had to deal with it. I started looking for new places but was severely restricted because of the boys' school and my employment. I did not want to change either of those two variables right then.

One afternoon while I was with Mr X, I received a phone call from an estate agent. After the call ended, Mr X asked if I was moving and I explained the situation. He was very quick to offer a solution which was mutually beneficial. He was living with his sister at the time and offered to find a home for us in a nearby town. Now this would not be the first time, he had made similar offers to me.

In 2011, he had promised a home in a posh county and, to show how serious he was, he even enrolled Son 2 in a private school nearby and we spent months looking for houses that never materialised. In fact he ran off leaving me with school fees in excess of four thousand pounds. Only the threat of a court action forced him to pay the outstanding amounts.

I was still blessed to be offered a solution but I was not particularly inclined. The offer from Mr X did not even make it to the table for my consideration before it was flatly rejected, burned and cursed three times over to ensure it was never mentioned again. I think this was my inner child trying to tell me something.

*****

To get a better understanding of why I had such strong emotions when it came to Mr X it may be prudent to give a quick history lesson to provide you with some context. Let me briefly explain how we met and how we had started our unconventional relationship some years before. We had met, not in the usual fashion but via a dating website. .

I had made the decision that I would go for the exact opposite of everyone else I had ever dated before, except for one condition: I was not prepared to go for anyone shorter than myself. Five feet and eight inches was my absolute compromise. A very shallow decision but an honest one.

This time I did not want anyone in my age group, no one that was considered stereotypically handsome, as long as I did not feel as if everyday was Halloween I could deal with even physical deformity. I wanted someone who was God-fearing and family-oriented, money did not matter.

After weeks of waiting to meet someone, a friend of mine advised me to try internet dating. I reluctantly and secretly signed up to a dating website. I quickly eliminated the usual suspects and went for the opposite of my past relationships. I started checking out my prospects. I quickly eliminated the people I would normally date. I did not have to feel any attraction for the person I chose. Arranged marriages worked so I figured I could make this one work. I chose Mr X because he matched my criteria the closest.

On more than one occasion he expressed his disbelief

he was actually dating me. It was perfect, because I knew or thought I knew that as long as he believed he was the luckiest man alive I did not need to worry about the usual relationship issues. I could focus on just being myself and chasing my dreams. I was never bothered too much by what others thought and when some of my friends expressed shock, horror, concern and other emotions I just ignored them and went ahead with my life. 'Is he rich?' they would ask and I would calmly tell them 'no'. They puzzled over my choice but I said and did nothing. It was my choice.

My mother who was never afraid to voice her opinion, whether it was needed or not, bluntly told me one afternoon to get rid of Mr X a day after he had stopped by to visit her. 'Where would you take this man?' she asked. ' He looks older than my own father.' But I would not be convinced to dump him although my family tried to reason with me, bribe and even threaten me.

I was quick to remind my family of my past relationships that had not worked out. I did not want to keep trying to find my Mr Right, I was satisfied with Mr *Maybe* and I intended to stick with my choice. 'My spirit just does not like him,' Mom would often say, but children at the best of times do not listen to their parents and usually end up suffering the consequences, which I certainly did.

A few months into our relationship I fell pregnant and that is when it all started to unravel. I was informed by Mr X that he was the eldest male in his family and could not have a child without the proper African courtship.

I very quickly realised that sometimes the packaging

does not have the correct labels and nine out of ten times people revert to their default settings. Unfortunately for me that meant an ancient outdated tradition where his entire family was involved in every decision-making process and women, I felt, were to be seen and not heard. This was an alien principle to a Jamaican woman. Most Jamaican women are usually heard before they are seen.

He suggested marriage but the idea just did not feel right. When I rejected his proposal I was called to his sister's home and told that I needed to terminate the pregnancy. I was horrified and in tears. Mr X then told me he would never accept my child nor would he sign any birth certificate. So our relationship suffered an untimely demise as I could not survive under the regime that I suddenly became subjected to nor could I terminate my child. It was not a moral decision, I just felt as if I had to have my child.

Though a lot more happened leading up to this point, I prefer to leave that for the sequel and drag you into the years that matter: 2016 and 2017. So allow me to take you back to the end of 2016.

Chapter 4
Not all that glitters is gold!

'Dreams do come true but sometimes it is just an illusion to mask a nightmare that may yet unfold
Not all that glitter is gold is an old prover, from childhood I have been told
For the world can be a horrible place and some hearts like stones are hard and cold.
Lessons we must learn in this world, although harsh, before we all grow old.

After a few months with no success in finding a home, in desperation I decided I might have to revisit Mr X's offer.

Mr X was excited and quickly upped his offer to a home that he would purchase cash with no mortgage and although I was still tentative and apprehensive based on my past experiences with him, I decided to accept his offer in the short term until I could sort myself out. I knew he was a liar, unreliable and a so-called player but he seemed to have turned a new page. He became very caring and started helping out with the boys more and more. He constantly updated me on paperwork that seemed legitimate and a bit of trust started to be built.

Instead of hiding from his responsibilities as he had done in the past, he seemed to be taking an active role in my boys' lives. My eldest son however was still wary as he had been hurt by Mr X before. There were no pleasantries, and conversations between the two were limited and somewhat strained. Having recognised my son's hesitation and knowing that I would never do anything to upset my children or make them feel threatened or uncomfortable, Mr X launched his charm offensive.

We were all invited to holiday in the south of England. Once there, the children were spoilt rotten by Mr X. My eldest was even taken out to play golf one-on-one with Mr X. They could stay up late, eat junk and just be children. My sister was even invited to join us. Mr X paid for everything. He refused to accept any monetary contributions. They loved it and the ice started to slowly melt. Little by little we realised that he might actually be different this time. Maybe older age had softened him a bit and he was becoming a nicer person. Everyone can change and everyone deserves a second chance, I thought.

When we returned from holidays, my sons and I were unpacking our bags upstairs when I asked my sons what they thought about Mr X. Son 1 still had concerns - he was the most intuitive - but decided that everyone needed another chance. I explained to my boys that I would never do anything to put them in danger or make them unhappy. All three reassured me that they knew and that they loved me. I rubbed the head of my eldest, scratched the head of my middle son and patted the head of my youngest son. It was an on-going joke between us.

I returned downstairs and I offered Mr X a cup of tea. After he had finished drinking his tea Mr X went to his vehicle, came back and offered me a brochure and some paperwork to look at. His offer went from getting a three-bedroom accommodation to purchasing a five-bedroom home for nearly half-a-million pounds, cash. I stood there in stunned silence and in complete shock in the middle of my lounge. For a solid minute I said nothing, not one word. I am not sure if I was even breathing during that minute because as soon I came back to reality I immediately had to take a sharp deep breath.

Not many things shock me but this one rendered me speechless for that moment. Clarity quickly returned and I sat down staring at Mr X suspiciously. Who would buy a house for half a million just to seek revenge on someone or invest that sum of money just to help an ex. It just did not make sense as the logical mind tried desperately to override the emotional mind.

Everything was moving too fast. I had to think and that meant I had to sleep. I hurriedly gave Mr X a random excuse and I bade him goodnight. I showered then checked that the boys were all in bed. They were always trying to sneak a few extra minutes on some electronic device.

Only Son 1 was up, the others were left exhausted by the long drive. I rubbed his head once again and headed to my room. A million random thoughts danced through my mind. What should I do? I played out so many possible scenarios, and before I realised or arrived at any conclusion I fell soundly asleep.

I woke up the next morning still feeling indecisive and exhausted because I had been restless all night. After the usual morning activities and two large cups of coffee later, I rang Mr X as I felt at this point I had to say something and at least establish conditions and boundaries before we proceeded, if I decided to proceed. I heard when the phone was connected but I didn't speak at first, I couldn't. There was a huge lump in my throat.

'Hello?' came the voice at the other end. I asked him if he could please pass by sometime during the day to have a talk. He asked if everything was okay and I responded that everything was great. He suggested about 3 pm and I agreed to meet him at my home and I hung up my mobile phone. I felt comfortable in my own space and if the meeting turned sour I could always show him the door.

After breakfast I asked my sister to take the boys out for a meal and then spend some time at the park as I needed to think in silence and plus I wanted to have a straight conversation with Mr X with no interruptions.

At about 3:10 pm my doorbell rang. I drew a deep breath and walked from the living room to my front door. He was elegantly dressed as usual in a crisp suit and that familiar smell. We kissed on both cheeks and I stepped inside to allow him room to follow. I made my way to the lounge and sat on the sofa and he sat down next to me. I half turned to face him and unconsciously rearranged the cushions to create a barrier between us and provide some support.

'Thank you for coming over. I just wanted to, ahhhm, ask a few questions. I mean what exactly is this?' and stopped to swallow after a huge lump that seemed to form in my throat yet again. I cleared my throat trying to dislodge it and I continued. 'What are your expectations?'

He opened his mouth to speak but before he could speak, I started laying out my conditions. Though I cannot remember the exact words used, the sentiments conveyed were as such: 'Mr X, I am not in love with you and I never will be. I love you and care for you but I am not in love with you. I know people do things and hope feelings and emotions may one day change but I know with absolute certainty that mine will never change. At my age I know what I am looking for.' I paused for a few seconds and he said nothing so I continued talking to fill the silence. 'At this point in my life, I don't want any drama. I just want peace so I can focus on my dreams.' He still said nothing. I changed my tactics and decided to ask some questions. 'Mr X, I need to ask you four things:

1. I currently live with my sister and I won't leave her behind, is there any place for her at this new house?
2. I will never give up on my dreams and that involves a lot of travelling and it is time consuming. Do you understand?
3. Living in this expensive home, what would you require me to contribute in terms of money?
4. Finally, do you understand that this will not be my permanent home in the long term?

Mr X replied to all my questions positively but as an after-thought I asked him to write it down, he hesitated then wrote it down. It was one of the few moments of genius inspiration I have ever had. A few moments later when he excused himself to use the bathroom I quickly snapped a photograph of the handwritten note, a move that I came to appreciate later in life.

When Mr X returned I told him that we would move

into the house he offered. He was absolutely elated and gave me a great big hug. Once again I reminded him that we were not entering into a relationship; it was merely an arrangement until I could sort my affairs and he agreed without any arguments.

*****

Over the next few weeks, occasionally a feeling of dread would revisit me and I would hesitate to do some task that I needed to get done so we could move house quickly or I would delay in making some appointments without any rational reason. I would stop frequently and think about the big decision I was about to make in my life. Not only in my life but my children's life.

On reflection I now believe that sometimes the universe tries to communicate with us but we become so preoccupied with other things, we ignore its subtle messages at our own peril. Those feelings of dread were more premonition than anxiety.

Being logic-minded, one day I sat down and literally wrote out the pros and cons of the decision I was about to make. This proved a futile exercise as the pros outnumbered the cons although the few cons I found had the potential to have a greater impact on my life forever. Here was my list:.

Pros

- I would live in an elegant five-bedroom house in a relatively posh area.
- My children would be safe.
- Financially I would not have to worry so much.
- My children would have some male influence.
- I could focus more on chasing my dreams.

Cons

- It was Mr X and he had a past.
- I would be at his mercy.

Since the pros won, I resumed packing in earnest.

We slowly drifted into a comfort zone and occasionally I would tell him I loved him because I did. It was not a passionate, earth moving love but a quiet appreciation for all he was doing. If I look back, I think this was the point I started making my first mistake and the lines became blurred. The boundaries between an ex-partner and girlfriend became blurred and we each assumed the role without any formality or conditions.

Mr X came by to drop off the keys to the new house in late October which made the move feel a little bit more real. It was really happening. I sat at the dining table with the keys in my hand and whispered a short invocation. Mr X stood there watching. 'Are you okay?' he asked. 'Don't tell me you're still having doubts, Vinette. What else can I do?' He sounded frustrated and I felt a sharp pangs of guilt. Recognising that he was trying, I changed my facial expression and gave him a huge smile.

I decided to, once again, outline the terms of our relationship: I loved him for all he was doing but I was not in love with him. We were not getting back together but I did promise him that I wouldn't date anyone for a while out of respect and if or when I found someone I would have to move. Those conditions suited him fine. He once again explained that there were five bedrooms: one for him, one for my sister, my eldest would have his own room, the two younger boys would share rooms and the other room would be mine. Argument settled we proceeded to look at the complete disarray in my lounge with opened boxes scattered throughout.

He looked around my living room. 'We need to take all these stuff to either a charity shop or dump them. I'll be buying you everything brand new.' I was back in panic mode. I looked about at 'my stuff'. Yes, they were just material things, just 'stuff', but more importantly they were 'my stuff, 'my kids' stuff', my past, my present; they were a part of me; they were things I had saved, and worked hard to buy. Each piece of furniture had a story or a memory that made me and helped to define who I am. I wouldn't say I was attached but they provided comfort and there was a certain peace knowing they were mine.

'I-I-I don't think I'm ready to get rid of my stuff,' I protested albeit weakly. 'What if. .?' I caught myself before I completed the sentence.

'What if what?' he enquired. 'Vinette, I've invested half-a-million pounds in a house for you and your kids. Are you telling me you still have 'what ifs'? Unbelievable! I can certainly afford to replace your furniture when you decide to move on.'

I noted that he had said '*your*' kids and not *our* kids, and a mini red flag was raised. I justified it as a mistake and brushed it to the back of my mind. I thought about this for a while but said nothing. 'Let's discusses this again please. Don't get upset,' I prompted. 'I just need to get my head straight! There are no expectations, right?'

'None whatsoever' he responded with zero emotional attachment as he rifled through a half-opened box by the kitchen door. He seemed totally uninterested in me. He looked at a plate I had in the box, smiled then turned and looked me in the eyes. 'Unless you want to,' he added. I shifted uncomfortably at the add on and giggled nervously but stepped away from his gaze.

'Do you expect any type of monetary contributions?' I continued with my back turned towards him.

'Nope. It's a mortgage free house. We have surplus cash. I've already put all the bills in my name and I will open a joint account so you gave access to money without the need to ask.'

'What about my sister? I want her to live with me and my boys.'

'That is fine also. There are five bedrooms, more than enough space.' He answered in a robotic and monotonous voice. I turned to face him with squinted eyes. He paused and bit his lower lip. 'Look here, Vinette, why can't you just accept that I'm being nice instead of trying to find problems where none exist. You're a lovely woman and I just want to treat you right. I messed up years ago and I would like to make amends.' He moved towards me and held me by both shoulders looking me straight in the eyes. He explained that he was not as close to his daughters as he would have liked and even shared that he did not attend his eldest daughter's wedding. He wanted to make sure he did right by Son 3 and build a relationship with him. I believed him because Son 3 was five years old but had never met either sibling.

'I understand but trust is slow to come back' I replied.

'Ok!' he said with a slight bit of irritation in his voice that made me furrow my brows and tilt my head to the right side. He immediately realised that I had picked up on his expression and smiled broadly which made the hairs on the back of my neck stand up. I quickly brushed my feelings aside and gave him a quick hug. It felt unnatural. I smiled.

Over the next few days I started packing what I needed to take and putting aside stuff I could discard. You never know how many things you have acquired each day until it is time to move. As I watched the pile of boxes growing and the house appearing more and more bare each day, I was suffering frequent panic attacks but I would not let it show. On the surface I thought I was happy, but inside my heart was beating erratically and my mind was all over the place.

Once again, a few weeks later, in a last minute bid by my common sense I called Mr X and insisted that I was going to keep some of my possessions. You could hear his frustration but I was adamant and I guess he sensed it and relented a bit. 'Ok, I tell you what,' he replied. 'I will ask my sister to keep your furniture, just in case. Ok?' he added with sarcasm.

'Yes, that sounds okay!' I breathed a sigh of relief as I knew I could at least have access to my furniture and 'stuff' if everything should go pear shaped. I felt more relaxed.

*****

Mr X rented a van and dumped the smaller items like garden chairs, old toys, clothes, small kitchen appliances and other miscellaneous items. I moved my refrigerator, all my solid wood furniture including bookcases, centre tables, a 50-inch television, centre tables, five beds, centre table, leather recliners, my beautiful glass six-seater dining table and chairs, utensils, drapes and numerous other items.

During the next few weeks of packing, Mr X was busy renovating the house. On a few occasions I was invited to contribute to a few trivial decorative decisions. He would listen intently but when I returned he had overruled all my choices. I said nothing as this was his area of expertise and it was not my house so I quietly stopped contributing. Another mini red flag was raised but I promptly brushed it to the back of my mind as there were so many other things happening in my life.

Work was becoming stressful once again. Just recently I was called into my boss's office, for sitting in a chair at the back of a meeting instead of at the front as he had instructed. I was also told off because I led an assembly instead of allowing my class to do it themselves. He was so full of himself - to the point that he once told the entire staff they were lucky they were working in this school because parents in his area were more concerned about their children's education. I remember shock and surprise on staff members' faces when in one meeting he stood sorrowfully and declared the wife of a staff member had died as if he was very close to the member of staff - only to be publicly corrected that the man's wife was very much alive.

My life was moving quickly and some days I struggled to keep up. Mr X busied himself getting the house ready. I had to move by November when my tenancy was up. I regularly visited the new house to check on how the work was progress and got to see Mr X other personalities on full display. His relationship with his workers opened my eyes to a different persona.

He changed the working contract he had made with the original renovators so many times that I firmly believe the company ended up losing money on the entire project but I thought to myself, I know nothing about the business world. In his original contract there was no clothes washer or dryer included, neither were there chrome sockets or door handles. I know for a fact, as I was there when the decisions were made at their offices. However, he insisted that they had been included and they had to find a way to get it done otherwise he would not pay. As soon as they completed any aspect of their work, he would walk around with little yellow dots or post-its to snag anything that was not to his liking. I would walk in the house and it would be covered in little yellow and red dots for months on end. I used to joke about those post-it notes and stickers … until they later became comments and instructions directed at my sons and myself.

In hindsight, and as I am writing this, it was all so obvious that this was a mistake but it is always easier to see things straight after the fact. When we are in a situation sometimes, we justify things our own minds, ignoring the obvious or subtle signs provided by the universe. I firmly believe that life is just a great big classroom and we learn everyday. My lesson was painful but I know that this would never happen to me again.

Chapter 5
The bank

I sat across from the bank employee and winced internally as he looked at me then looked at Mr X. I could read his mind to the very comma and full stop.

He wanted to know why I was with this man? He would not be a good poker player as his facial expressions gave away every thought that had crossed his mind. Though to be honest, it was not the first time I had encountered questioning looks whenever we were together; I expected it. I read the conclusion that he had drawn. He decided I was in it for the money, and he nodded imperceptibly to confirm to himself that he was indeed correct. I said nothing, I just smiled, but my eyes remained cold and staring at him, His eyes met mine and he shifted uncomfortably then looked away.

He knew I knew his very thoughts and he suddenly became self conscious. Mr X said nothing to indicate he knew about the silent conversation that had just occurred between the bank employee and myself. I momentarily wondered if he had ever observed the questioning eyes and puzzled expressions that greeted us sometimes. I looked at him but he seemed oblivious. I quickly recalled a visit to an acupuncturist where the person behind the counter greeted him and enquired if I was his daughter. He shot daggers at the man and I had secretly smiled inside. I have long held the belief that people's outward appearances are heavily influenced by the inside. If you are an evil person it eventually shows on the surface and you start to look old and haggard.

Mr X described the joint account he wanted and I nodded in agreement, no thought, energy or effort was required from me and I gave none. 'There's one thing!' the bank clerk interjected. 'Since Mr X already has accounts at this bank, I had to commit to pay in £1000.00 each month as the money needed to come from another source, not be transferred from another account.'

I shifted uncomfortably in my seat. I had no idea why. Mr X spoke up: 'you can just put your salary in this account and withdraw it again. We are a family hon.' He smiled and reached out to put his arms around me pulling me closer and I unconsciously flinched and moved away from his grasp.

I noticed that once again the clerk's mind had started to wander with the same questions but this time a few doubts had crept in by my reaction. 'Why did she flinch?' the clerk was asking himself. If I was in it for the money, why was he asking for my salary to be paid into this account? It didn't quite add up in his mind, but once again he ended with the same conclusion. This time he deliberately avoided my eyes and started shuffling papers to distract my steady, icy gaze.

'Whatever,' I thought to myself. Then my thoughts drifted slowly back to the decision to put all my income in one account with Mr X's name on it. I didn't like the idea but for some strange reason I said nothing. I would also ask him about us being a family.

Once outside before I even spoke, Mr X explained

without any prompts that he said family because it would just make it easier to open the account without the usual questions or possible reference checks since he had banked there for years.

*****

Weeks after, in late December 2016, Mr X approached me to ask why my salary was not reflected in the joint account. I told him explicitly that I felt uncomfortable with the arrangement and would rather keep my account separate then transfer money o help with the bills, even though he had not asked for any help. He gave me one of those steely gazes and I felt the urge to explain myself.

'I still have the cable, internet and phone bills,' I muttered and it comes from my home account.

'Well, let me set up those accounts on this account then,' he replied.

'But what if I need a bill in my name?' I queried.

'Vinette,' he held me by both shoulders, 'let me take care of you. Relax, you've always been alone doing everything for yourself. Allow me to be a man to you. You do not need bills in your name, everything is sorted. This is your home for as long as you choose.'

Immediately I felt guilty. Maybe I was too caught up being single and could not embrace what it meant to be taken care of for a while. I smiled and hugged him. He was after all doing a lot for me and my children. I decided to just close my account and put everything in Mr X 'joint account that weekend. Saturday morning came and I had all I needed to head to the bank and close my account. I got in my car, then suddenly remembered that the bank had sent the new cards for the joint account a few days before with a chequebook. I had opened both letters with the card and the activation code and left it inside my bedside drawer. I rushed upstairs to collect it but it was nowhere to be found. I checked everywhere but it was gone. Did I misplace it? I thought I'd ring the bank to cancel the card but I would check if Mr X had seen it first.

I dialled Mr X's number to ask him if he had seen it but at the last minute decided against it and hung up the phone quickly. That odd feeling came back again. I cannot quite describe it, it was a pervading sense of uneasiness and anxiety. I went into My X's room and opened his chest of drawers and searched through each drawer. I got to the last drawer and instinctively put my hand over my open mouth to stifle any sound that might escape involuntarily. Lying in the bottom drawer under some folders were the missing bank card, activation letter and cheque book. I closed the drawer and said nothing.

Did he accidentally place it there, believing it was his own? Was he keeping it safe for me? I asked myself these innocent questions but I sensed something deeper and more sinister but was afraid to ask deeper questions and afraid to get the answers I subconsciously knew.

Weeks later I went back to check and realised they had been moved. I never saw either the bank card, PIN number or any other correspondence relating to the account ever again. However a month later Mr X invited me to sign a cheque to pay for a school trip.

Looking back, I supposed he wanted to make sure that I had used the account at least once but I never got the chance to even activate the bank card and was denied access to the joint account even though I started putting money into it.

Chapter 6
Cracks to Craters

There's not that much to see
take it from me
That tiny break is just a tiny crack
everything else remains intact
from a distance it all looks so wholesome and good
exactly how a family normally would
but closer and what you see is not what it infers
tiny cracks are actually deep craters

About three weeks after moving in I began to realise I had made a terrible mistake.

My first major alert was my sons' behaviour. My first two sons started to change drastically. Son 1 became more and more withdrawn and would hide in his room for hours. He suffered from Asperger's and was more perceptive and easily stressed. Whenever he was placed in difficult or uncomfortable situations he would retreat to his room instead of confiding in anyone.

Son 2 became timid and withdrawn. He was always the loudest and most sporty of the three boys but in a few weeks his voice almost completely disappeared, his shoulders hunched and he was always looking downwards; only Son 3 was happy, partly because Mr X kept telling him that he was the boss. Son 3 had changed too. He became more confident and started becoming more obnoxious to his brothers and on many occasions I had to be quite stern with him. I started to see cracks appearing where strong brotherly bonds existed before.

I knew then, I had to move soon. I spoke with my sons but they would not complain, I guess to protect me. I decided to start saving in earnest to move out as quickly as I could.

I explained one afternoon to Mr X that I was feeling uncomfortable and would move out soon and that is when Mr X started changing everything. He approached me one afternoon and suggested I should quit my job and he would offer me £30,000 to start my own business as he knew that's what I wanted to do. Somehow I was not even tempted. I had quit my job before at his request and ended up on benefits when he walked away because I did not do as I was told. Months later he would tell a judge under oath that I had taken this money in lieu of unpaid child support.

I quickly realised he was the same sadistic person he always was. He had not changed but now I was trapped. All my belongings were taken, I was living in his house and I had limited savings. Realising he had me between a rock and a hard place, he started laying down rules after rules, not just for the children but even for me as an adult. We would all be called to give account if any of the rules were ever violated. Our bins and handbags were searched and we had to give account. We were not allowed to consume certain foods and we were forbidden from entering certain spaces. Only Son 3 was allowed to do as he please.

He gathered us all one afternoon to lay down the rules of living in HIS house. I felt embarrassed and completely humiliated. At the end of his lecture he told us if we didn't like it we could go but I had to leave Son 3 behind as he would file for custody and since I did not have a home or furniture, any judge would file in his favour. For the first time I felt real panic. I could not risk losing my son and somehow I irrationally mentally assumed he was right and locked myself in my own mental prison. I could not lose my child.

The next few weeks became harder and harder and, as my options were limited, I countered and became nicer and nicer to soften his edges and make life a little more tolerable for everyone else. I felt it was all my fault for getting my children and my sister into the situation and it ate at me day and night. Mr X behaved like a king. His sister also got into the act whenever she visited and I felt completely trapped.

I did as I was told and I tried to be as nice as possible. Somewhere in the process all the lines and boundaries became more blurred. I was pretending now to be the loving girlfriend just to make life easier for everyone as I felt it was all my fault. I wanted to make sure my children were happy and so I forgot about my happiness in the process. I would smile with Mr X, hug and kiss him, send flirtatious texts, b and in return I would get days and, if I was lucky weeks, of peace and time to plan.

Mr X basked in his new found power. He would slap me on my bottom, touch me whenever he had the chance and

I would playfully push him away, desperately trying not to anger or upset him. My life had descended into hell but I kept up the pretence and kept smiling. My only escape was writing and Toastmasters, my speaking club. I was also an active Rotarian until Mr X found out it was mostly men and I decided to quit abruptly after a few unsavoury comments. By now I was suffering from a persistent headache that just wouldn't go. A quick visit to my doctor confirmed that my blood pressure had skyrocketed and I was placed on medication immediately.

*****

I came home one evening after a meeting to find Son 2 timidly waiting at the door, nervously peeking around to see if he was being watched. It broke my heart to see his slumping shoulders and big sad eyes. His face brightened as soon as he saw me, 'Mom,' he said devoid of any real joy but with a soft smile on his lips and eyes that hid deep sadness and pain that made a mother's heart bleed. He came straight into my arms. 'I'm glad you're home!' He hugged me tightly and I hugged him tighter. I could feel the tears stinging the corners of my eyes and I struggled to hold them back. Then we heard the footsteps on the wood floor coming from the back of the house and he tensed in my arms and attempted to pull away looking down at his toes. I pulled him back into my arms and held him even tighter, hugging him to my chest unconsciously to protect him and keep him safe.

Mr X appeared around the corner and chuckled at the sight of us standing there. It has always been difficult for me to try to explain to anyone the feeling that comes over the entire house when he chuckles. I could feel my body tensing and mentally forced myself to relax. I smiled. 'Good evening,' I could hear my voice as I spoke and could detect the subdued tone and wariness in it.

'What's this then?' He stopped and pushed his chin out towards us, arms akimbo and within a few feet. My son once again tried to pull away and once again I pulled him back.

'I'm giving my son a cuddle,' I answered in an alien voice.

'Shouldn't he be doing his homework?' he continued.

'As soon as I finished cuddling him,' I replied with a little more bite to my voice this time.

He stood there as if waiting for me to let go but I was determined not to move first. 'How long does a cuddle last?' he questioned after he realised I had no intention of letting my son go to please him.

'As long as I want it to last,' I replied and closed my eyes drawing my son tightly to my body and rocking gently back and forth. I could not hear any movement so I knew he was still standing there waiting.

I slowly opened my eyes, held Son 2 at arms length and looked him straight in the eyes. 'I know baby and I love you always.' I kissed him on the forehead and he turned to walk away but Mr X was blocking his path. He loved doing that, for people to either wait around or ask him to pass. Somehow he thought it gave him some type of power.

*****

We were not the only victims of this practice. Once

he had ordered some office furniture from a company to be delivered and installed. The salesmen drove over one hundred miles to get to the house. After some discussions between Mr X and the company staff on the drive, the men started unloading the furniture pieces. He stood there watching them unload the pieces as they rushed around to beat the rain that was spitting. After they had completely unloaded everything on the drive, Mr X informed them he needed to get a broom from his garage that was now being blocked by the furniture that was just unloaded. 'Could we just check it off then move it to the office?' the worker asked pleadingly, realising that they might need to put everything back on the truck and unload it a second time.

'No!' He chuckled. 'I need my broom now.' The worker looked at him in disbelief but a client is a client so they packed the furniture back into the van, allowed Mr X to get his broom then unloaded again, checked the pieces then moved the pieces into the office.

I believed he thought these actions gave him power, Money may buy material things but it certainly does not buy class or the ability to empathise with others.

*****

Neither my son nor I spoke. We just stood there with eyes lowered before he finally decided to move and we walked past him towards the second reception room. 'No hugs for me? ' he queried, his voice threatening and nasty. I hated touching him; he repulsed me. Nevertheless I needed a roof and plus I needed to figure out a way to get my furniture back from his sister's house first. I stiffy turned and planted that fake smile on my lips and robotically gave him a hug. He grabbed onto me tightly and my arms dropped to my side but still he held onto me. I didn't want to upset him so I just stood there as if lifeless. 'So, your son gets a long tight hug and I get this?' he asked menacingly.

'I'm just a bit tired,' I tried to explain and slowly disengaged from his arms.

He held me at arms length and laughed out loud. 'Too tired to hug me, but not tired to hug your son. Ah Vinette! Vinette! Vinette !' And then he gave me a look that said trouble was coming. The hairs on the back of my neck were standing on end. I turned and followed Son 2 to the second reception room where he stood hiding behind the door.

'Mom can you please pick me up from school tomorrow?' he whispered. The desperate plea in his eyes meant I could only give one answer.

'Yes hon!' I replied with a smile and rubbed his head. I threw my arms around him and we headed to the kitchen, arm in arm. We were not allowed to use the door to directly enter the kitchen but had to walk the long way around.

*****

I got up the next day at my usual 5 am and quickly collected my bedding from the sofa where I now slept and moved quickly and quietly up the stairs so the children did not realise I was sleeping downstairs: my room was too close to Mr X and the doors had no locks. Nothing had happened but I had an intense feeling of foreboding and could not sleep soundly at nights. I would wake up at every tiny nondescript sound each night, so after everyone was in bed I would slowly creep downstairs with my duvet and a pillow and sleep there. I would wake up early in the morning and make my way upstairs before anyone else was awake.

I headed up to my room to put my sheets and pillows away and was surprised by Mr X coming down the stairs dressed in his golf regalia. I gasped but he didn't look one bit surprised or concerned that I was midway up the stairs with my pillow and duvet in hand. After regaining my composure, I smirked because I knew he thought he looked good and believed the world shared this skewed opinion but I said nothing. 'Morning,' I muttered, yawning and pretending to be sleepier than I was.

'Good morning,' he cheerily replied, 'off to play golf all day. Will you miss me?'

'Of course hon,' I offered the obligatory lie. I am sure by now we both realised it was a lie but still we kept up the pretence for civility. As I passed him he leaned over for a kiss and I offered him my cheek. He smiled and I suddenly became nervous once again but couldn't figure out why. I squeezed passed him and he slapped me on the behind murmuring, 'later' which made the hairs in the back on my neck stand up and sent a shiver up my spine. A missed step caused me to momentarily lose my balance and I quickly caught myself before I fell. 'Try not to touch the walls,' he scolded from the bottom of the stairs, 'they're white.' 'Sorry ' I replied without looking back.

*****

I started to become a bit more anxious about my children

when I was not at home and so under the guise that my mom was ill, I managed to convince Mr X to allow her to visit for a while. I did not let mom know the real reasons behind the invitation. My mother is wonderful and if one of her children needed any help, they only needed to ask and she would be there.

I asked and she promised to come in a few weeks. I was grateful when she arrived.

*****

The first incident happened sometime in late December 2016 or January 2017 as far as I can recollect. I have blocked so much out in trying to rebuild myself and who I was that I am no longer sure exactly when.

I was putting clothes on Mr X's bed when he came into the room and locked the door behind him.

I did not move.

I did not fight.

But I cried.

Chapter 7
Trouble starts to brew

Simmer, simmer, boil then bubble
the atmosphere is ripe for expected troubles
Like thick, dark clouds rising in gloom
the devil ruthlessly plan and conspires.

The email arrived just as I sat down in the staffroom at work. My phone was on silent so it just vibrated in my jacket pocket. Always my first instinct when a message, text or email comes in was, 'are my children okay?'

I slyly glanced at my phone to see who had contacted me. I did not want other staff members to see my reaction. I had to keep my air of confidence and the smile that protected me from prying questions and the inevitable rumours that might follow. Human beings operate in a connect-the-dots world in order to make sense of everything. If there is a missing dot in the picture, then some search and try to find it but the majority simply put 'I' in its place disregarding its impact. They make up any story to complete their picture.

The notification said it was Mr X and my heart immediately skipped a nervous beat. What now? I thought as I nervously recalled what had happened in the morning before work. Had I left something out of place? Did one of the children say or do something wrong? I started imagining all the worst possible scenarios.

I didn't even realise nor can I pinpoint the exact moment

I became so fearful and anxious. It just gradually crept up on me. How quickly I had learned to mask my emotions too. On the surface I appeared to everyone as independent, calm and ambitious. I dread to think how many women may have subconsciously wished they were in my position without knowing the hell I was going through in my personal life.

I decided not to read the email that moment. Scared that whatever message it contained may affect my entire day and I had a full day at work. By 9 am I realised I could barely focus and pretty soon my nerves got the better of me. I sent for a colleague who was passing by to call a technician and lied that I urgently needed the toilet. I asked her to stay in my laboratory for five minutes and I rushed to my locker to grab my phone then headed to the toilet. I bolted myself in the cubicle and nervously opened my phone fearing the worst.

The picture downloaded first, it was a picture of a coke bottle with the caption, 'I wonder what's the explanation for this?' A seemingly innocent statement but it was more than that. Mr X had gone into my sister's bedroom and rummaged through her garbage bin, found a coke bottle, placed it on her bed then took the picture to send to me. A small tear ran down my cheek as I looked up and whispered, 'God, let this be over soon'. I just sat in the toilet for a minute then dried my face and flushed the toilet just in case someone was next door. I checked the mirror then painted on my smile again and walked back to my lesson.

'You ok?' Ms W asked.

'Yeah,' I joked, 'too much coffee' and started laughing loudly to show the triviality of the situation. I decided I would start worrying later, on my way to the house.

I somehow managed to finish that day without any further major incident. At the end of the day, as usual, I raced away from work, anxious to get home because I was now the buffer between Mr X and my children. I felt like the sea walls that are designed to protect from the land from the sea but I was grateful I did not look like what I was going through.

I was parked outside Son 1's school, waiting for him so as to rush to the house and be there for the other two boys. I felt the vibration in my jacket pocket and hurriedly glanced at my phone. It was Mr X again. I took a deep breath and answered, 'hello!'

'Send me a dirty text'

'No!'

'Come on, send me one. Tell me how much you want me. Make it sound real. Don't be a prude.'

'Yes, I want you badly. I want you to make me sweat,' I said, swallowing my own vomit. 'Dirtier,' he ordered, 'and text it to me.' He hung up and I did as instructed. This would become a routine and I would comply for a few days of peace. He knew he had me between a rock and a hard place. Nowhere to go and with no extra money saved, he would take my son and I would do anything before that happened.

I drove home slowly. I would rather be anywhere, going anywhere or sleeping anywhere else tonight. Just one night of peace. It was the same each evening. I would drive slowly down the road, praying that his vehicle was not on the drive. This evening was no different. I could physically feel my heart pounding through my chest. I leaned forward in my seat to peer around the corner and my heart sank. His vehicle was parked on the drive like a big black ominous cloud. I slowly drove unto the drive, not wanting to alert anyone that I was home. Every muscle in my entire body was so tense they physically ached.

I sat quietly, switched off my engine, leaned back and closed my eyes, willing my body and mind to get the strength needed to go inside. Son 1 said nothing, he too sat in silence staring at the house. I sensed a movement in the shadows of the house and turned my head to see him, standing there staring at us. He had appeared at the side gate with a broom in his hand. I smiled nervously and felt the need to explain myself. I quickly wound my window down. 'Hi, how was your day, hon? I had a long day, just feeling tired. I love you !' I opened the door, embraced him and offered a quick peck on his cheek. I was speaking a mile a minute and just rattling words almost incoherently. Son 1 opened his door quickly and used the few seconds of distraction to rush into the house.

'It really does not look good to the neighbours when you sit out here on the drive,' he replied.

'Sorry, I was just tired, that's all.'

'You should go inside then,' he replied.

'I will next time, sorry,' I apologised.

I hastily collected my bag and went inside. Leaving him

standing at the side gate staring after me. I gently closed the door as we had been repeatedly warned not to slam the door as the whole house would shake. I quickly removed my shoes so I would not get dirt inside and stored them where they belonged, making sure the closet door was properly closed behind me. I then quietly went into the lounge to put my bags down in the place I was told to put them.

'Mom?' a small voice whispered from upstairs. 'Is that you?'

'Yes baby. Are you ok'

'Yes,' Son 2 timidly whispered but his body language and the tone of his voice suggested that he was not.

I tried to tell him I loved him but a big lump blocked my voice and all I could offer was a smile. I walked lightly up the stairs meeting him halfway and wrapped my arms around him. Son 2 had lost his vibrancy and was like a shadow of his usual boisterous self. What had I done to my child? I needed to get away. I was scared of asking his sister for my furniture without alerting Mr X about my intentions before I was ready to go so I said nothing.

I briefly thought about a shelter but hastily dismissed the thought. I think because of pride and embarrassment for myself and children. I might even lose my children. The risk was too great.

*****

That night Mr X walked into the lounge where I was lying down in the darkness, once again pretending to sleep. I felt my body go rigid and my limbs stiffened and I started breathing heavily pretending to snore and hoping he was just passing through to get something from the kitchen. I knew he was not, but maybe tonight he would leave me alone. He stood there allowing his eyes to get acclimated to the darkness, then he quietly closed the reception door behind him and I knew what was coming next.

The tears started forming and my heart started that rapid thumping. I snored even louder hoping it would not happen. He bent over the sofa I could smell his sugary breath from his diabetes. Sweet and sickly, I could feel his breath then his hands.

I erratically changed the pattern of my breathing like someone whose peaceful sleep has been disturbed and attempted to turn my body as if to settle into a new comfortable position. He paused as I rolled on my side with my back towards him but I could still sense his presence, it filled the entire room like a thick black cloud and I struggled to breathe. He sat on the sofa, the curve of my back providing support for his back.

'Stop pretending to sleep!' he whispered with a harshness to his voice.

I remained motionless with a steady breathing of someone lost in sleep and completely unaware.

'Wwwhat!'I muttered through a stifled yawn as I stretched, trying to keeping up the pretence. 'Are you ok?' I asked, pretending that I was drowsy and completely oblivious to my surroundings. I would do anything to change the course of events that were about to unfold although I knew it was pointless. I focussed on my children sleeping upstairs to stifle the strong reflex gag that threatened to engulf me. What choice did I have? I had no savings, no furniture, no house. At least for just tonight they had a roof over our heads.

My mind left my body. I imagined that I was a great speaker, loads of cash, many accolades. I imagined when I was a child back in Jamaica running to the sea each morning for fresh fish that the fishermen had just caught. These would be scaled and escoveitched to be eaten with boiled white yam for dinner. It was delicious. I imagined flying to exotic destinations. Living off the land, I imagined my phone call that would never end. I imagined I was at a party with my friends, laughing, singing and just being happy. How we laughed.

Then it was over and I was alone. I could taste the saltiness of my tears but heard no sound except the footsteps as the stairs creaked. I said nothing; I felt nothing. I waited until there was complete silence. Checked under my pillow for my mobile phone. It was 3:48 am. I started to write.

The bogey man

The bogey man he comes at night
When all is quiet and voices are still
His breath is sweet with that fruity smell
He caresses you and forces his will.
Oh the bogey man he wear a suit
With cotton shirts and shiny shoes
With air of gentry and golf a plenty
Foolish you'd be to dare accuse
The bogey smiles and wears a grin
It chills the bones and scares the weak
He looks through eyes that taunt and tease
Your spirit shudders and you cannot speak
The bogey man looks deep into you
And you hide yourself from his woeful stare
He'll makes your hair stand on their end
Each time you feel him drawing near!
He is the bogeyman, beware !

Chapter 8
Bigger cracks!

Ping! ping! went my phone and I glanced at the screen and I was immediately sorry I did. Sometimes it is better not to know so you can just carry on with your day in peace and wonderful blissful ignorance. It was from the bogeyman with the ominous words, 'we need to speak tonight.' My blood ran cold. He somehow always timed it when I got to work and my entire day would flow by in excruciating fearful expectation of what might or might not happen.

'What now?' I thought to myself as I mentally retraced what he could possibly want to talk about. I felt my throat tightening, my forehead tensing and my heart starting to beat rapidly, increasing with every step. What might I have done wrong? I couldn't find anything and panic began to set in. I could feel my throat tightening even more, my forehead tense and my heart beat a wild scattered rhythm.

Its funny looking back now that it never occurred to me that it might be something positive. It never was, except on the odd occasion he wanted to show someone how good he was. The bogeyman was cold and calculating and nothing he did was spontaneous. Everything was all planned with military precision.

By 10am I was already worrying about going home. I wanted to retrieve my phone from my locker again and check for messages but decided not to. It would only depress me further as it had done many other days prior. I drifted off into my head.

'Miss?' Student A called 'can you help me?'

I didn't hear a word. I was lost in my state of panic. A sense of foreboding descended on me and changed my mood. Sensing that I had lost focus, the small chatter in the background grew louder and louder until it attracted the attention of a passing colleague.

'Sorry miss, I didn't know you were in here. Are you ok?' Miss M said from the opened classroom door. I made eye contact and smiled. I didn't speak immediately because I was afraid the tears might be released. I drew a few deep breaths and when I was satisfied I was ready, I attempted an explanation.

'What? Oh yes yes, I am here. Group work.' I turned to the class. 'Enough now. Get back to your seats and be quiet.' I needed time to think and plan a strategy. I was in no mood for another episode again tonight but what else could I do?

The class sat in stunned silence. Not quite knowing how to proceed or exactly what to do. They had completed all the work set but didn't dare say another word, either because they were too lazy to bother or they were genuinely scared.

I looked at themthem; they looked at me. I shook my head; they looked away. Better not to face the beast. I glanced downwards, ashamed. They had done nothing but they had no idea what I was going through.

'Sorry,' I managed to mumble. 'I overreacted. Please take five minutes to pack away.'

I needed to stop thinking. I drifted through the rest

of the day and if you had asked me what happened a second before, I would not have been able to say. I was like a zombie. Nothing registered. I was just a smiling shell walking around. Finally, gratefully and worriedly the day ended and in the same zombie-like trance I numbly walked to my car.

At that moment a long sleep would have been an avenue for escape. I felt the familiar stinging at the inner corners of my eyes; it was a familiar feeling now, the tears threatening to burst free but being held back by pride, indifference and a numbness, numbness in my mind, my body and in my soul. It was a numbness as if my spirit had gone and left only the physical shell and nothing was inside. Nothing except a distant fire fuelled by love for my children. They were keeping me alive. There were the embers; they glowed and kept me alive. The sudden thought of my children dulled the stinging in my eyes and my lips curled into a smile at some memory that escaped for a moment and fanned the flames a bit higher.

I opened my car door, sat inside and allowed myself a brief respite as I recalled the day my middle son saw me in a black-and-white picture and innocently asked, 'Mom, in your day was the world in black and white?' I had laughed so much my sides hurt. Now the same emotions overtook my current situation and forced me to smile. I leaned back against the headrest, closed my eyes and allowed myself the brief escape and just embraced memory after memory after memory. It was a welcome interlude.

Voices in the distance interrupted my thoughts and I

opened my eyes without even leaning forward or moving my head, just my eyes moved and I realised other teachers were making their way to the car park. Not wanting to attract any unnecessary attention I sat up straight, started my car and drove slowly out.

I collected Son 1 from school and asked about his day, We chatted for a bit before he reclined in his seat and drifted off to sleep. We drove in complete silence. Eventually, I turned into the road that led to home, driving as slow as possible that would not attract any unnecessary attention.

A vehicle looking like the bogey mobile appeared in my rear-view mirror and I tensed and increased my speed but it was a false alarm. I slowed down again. I made the penultimate turn and once again I was so grateful for the speed bumps.

I had to drive slowly. Ten miles per hour seemed fast. Slowly I eased up off the accelerator, allowing the car to proceed in a forward direction on its own momentum. I was blank. After bump three the car tried to go over but it had lost momentum and rolled backwards. I did not try to stop it and just allowed it to roll back a few feet. By now my eyes were completely glazed over. Just one minute away was a whole new world. The sound of an engine caused me to glance in my rear-view mirror again. A car had appeared behind me once again. I held up my hands in apology and pulled to the side allowing him to pass by. I sat, one minute from home but a universe away from happiness and peace.

Son 1 stirred and adjusted his sleeping position. I scratched his head. ' I'm sorry,' I whispered. He stirred again and opened his eyes.

'Mom? Are you ok?'

'Yes hon.' I smiled and nodded.

'Are we home yet?'

'Almost.' He went back to sleep.

I drove past the house and saw the bogey mobile parked on the drive. I sat for about half-an-hour in the cul-de-sac. When Son 1 stirred again I turned the car around and drove to the house. I did not wait in the car this time after that encounter on the drive weeks ago. I woke Son 1 and hurriedly got out and opened the front door as quietly as possible and immediately Son 1 darted upstairs, rushed into his room and closed the door behind him.

Mr X suddenly appeared from the back of the house before I could follow and ordered me to come into the kitchen. I was barely into the kitchen when he spoke.

'Your child is no longer allowed in MY kitchen, effective immediately! Let him eat somewhere else and don't think any food will be allowed upstairs either!' he shouted at me even though I was standing just three feet away from him.

He wanted Son 1 to hear and everyone in the house. He was the authority as he regularly reminded us and no one would dare challenge him or they ran the risk of immediate eviction.

I stood there, numb all over. I felt the tears welling up in my eyes and I willed them away. 'W-w-why?' I stuttered.

'What did he do?'

'He opens my kitchen cupboards too often,' he replied.

'What?' I asked, puzzled and perplexed. Are you joking?

'This was unbelievable and I didn't know how to react or even feel. Who would ban a child from a kitchen? It suddenly became too much to bear. All my fears seemed to disappear and anger took over.

'You bastard!' I seethed. ' I hate you, I f*****ng hate you. You are a f****g bastard!' I repeated, pounding on the granite counter as the tears kept rolling down my cheeks. I was screaming at this point although no sound was coming out.

A normal person may have attempted to calm me down or argue back but he remained composed and managed to even muster a smile. He seemed pleased at my reaction and slowly walked away. I just stood there sobbing until all I could hear was each shallow breath I took. I consciously slowed my breathing as the tears continued streaming down my cheeks. The whole episode had lasted less than five minutes. I dried my tears with the back of my hands and the button at the end of my jacket snagged at my right eye. I blinked rapidly to ease the slight pain and only then did it register that I was alone.

There I was standing in the middle of the kitchen barefooted. I quickly wiped my eyes, adjusted my jacket, scanned the room for the monster. He was outside sitting on his bench talking. I could not hear what he was saying but he seemed as if he was having a great time, throwing his head back in laughter and wildly gesticulating. There was no sign that I was stood in the middle of the kitchen bawling my eyes out nor the fact that he had just banished my son from his kitchen. I just stood there staring blankly at him. He turned, caught my eye and smiled, his artificial teeth glinting.

I squinted at Mr X and gave him my middle finger which just resulted in a bigger smile. He found pleasure in his actions which made me even more upset. I was no longer upset at his actions but more upset that I allowed him to upset me and caused me to lose my control. I gave him a disapproving glance then blatantly opened the kitchen door that we were forbidden to use and walked right through it and I didn't care if he saw me. To prove my point, I left the door completely ajar. I made my way up the stairs to check on my boys. All were locked in one room. I smiled and said 'hey' just to gauge whether or not they had heard the commotion downstairs.

'Are you ok mom?' Son 2 asked. That told me they had heard everything.

I immediately felt ashamed because my children were not used to me swearing. I was about to lie but the look in their eyes told me not to. Even so I did not want to tell them the full truth; I had to protect them; they did nothing to deserve this. I decided to ask them bluntly, 'darlings are you all happy living here?'

'No,' came the responses without any hesitation. 'Can we please go Mom. It doesn't feel right.' And then the tears started flowing. My eldest put an arm around the others. Three pairs of sorrowful eyes looked to me and the tears slowly started streaming down my eyes as well.

'Give me a month, okay? Let me get some money together because we have lost everything, all my furniture, everything, but I promise. I will get you out of here. I am so sorry. Group hug!' We hugged for a few minutes until I could feel eyes burning into my back.

' What's this?' he asked.

' A family ' my eldest replied with indignation.

'A family?' he scoffed

'Yes, we have always been and will always be,' my eldest replied. I placed a calming hand on his shoulders as I sensed he was getting angry, which was completely out of character.

'You four, ha, a family,' he continued. We just sat all four of us looking at him. Somehow the united front made him aware that he was an outsider and a flicker of hurt registered on his face for a brief moment.

Son 3 shouted, 'Daddy you're mean; I love Mom a hundred times more than you.' He walked away without a word and disappeared into his room.

'I hate him so much,' Son 2 whispered.

'Don't hate baby. Don't let anyone change who you are.' I cuddled him and kissed his forehead.

It is funny the strength you find when your children are hurt. That early morning when Mr X appeared I was not going to accept it; I was going to fight and fight I did. I bashed him with a lamp and ran. The commotion woke the entire household and I immediately felt ashamed. I still couldn't bring myself to say what had initiated my outburst so instead I apologised. Instead of scaring Mr X, he knew that I would be too embarrassed to share what was happening so this became a new point of leverage for him.

The drive to work cleared my head and panic once again set in. I envisioned coming home with my clothes out on the drive. I quickly texted Mr X to apologise for hitting him. My heart ached and a huge lump formed in the back of my throat just looking at Son 1 as we drove together. His anguish was evident on his face although he desperately tried not to show it. He wanted to protect me from any more stress and although I was grateful, as a mother my heart bled. I was meant to protect him, not the reverse, and my smile temporarily dimmed. We drove in silence, both of us ignoring the obvious pain and angst and quickly discussed the weather and the beautiful sunrise. 'I love those colours!' he exclaimed, 'they're so warm and vibrant.' I was so glad to have a son who appreciated nature and all its wonderful offers. I smiled and held his hands. He gripped my hand tightly and a single tear escaped down my cheek.

'I love you,' I whispered hoarsely because the huge lump had formed at the back of my throat again. He squeezed tighter. We drove for miles in complete silence, each of us lost in our own thoughts, each of us dreading to go home that night. Each day was a complete uncertainty. Well, not completely uncertain because we knew there was going to be something negative, the only uncertainty was what form would it take that day.

*****

We made it through the day and on my drive home I stopped by the nearest KFC and bought us dinner.

I had to find time with Son 1 but I knew it was at the

expense of Son 2 who suffered quietly too until I could get home. Although mom was now around, I knew they wanted me but I was still grateful Mom was there to help me. I told her nothing, though I knew she sensed something was not right. I kept up the pretence.

I was being torn in so many different directions and it drained me and I felt broken inside. Reducing one child's suffering, increased it for another. I had to accept I could not be in two places at once; it was impossible physically and mentally and emotionally. I was running on empty and so my smile was just my hollow mask that I wore everywhere. My smile felt frozen, false and unfamiliar. The smile had left my eyes long ago but I remained hopeful it would return someday soon before I was completely spent.

We sat in the car together with minimal conversation.

'How was school today?'

'Good,' Son 1 replied after swallowing his mouthful of chicken. We engaged in casual conversation then drove slowly home. There was never any rush to go home. Traffic jams were a welcome occurrence any day of the week.

The hardest part of the journey was always that last turn. The joy of ourr entire day depended on that turn. Would his vehicle be there or gone? If it was gone an immediate relief washed over the entire household. The car crept slowly and we pushed our heads forward in unrehearsed unity to see around the corner before the entire car got there. We were out of luck that day, again. His vehicle was there - big, black and ominous like a hearse - and our undertaker was waiting inside.

We just parked on the drive and sat there forgetting our instructions. Neither of us spoke or even attempted to leave my car. We didn't even move; it felt as if we didn't move we would be okay. We glanced nervously to the side of the house expecting an appearance but none came and we were grateful. Nothing eventful occurred and I began to worry even more.

*****

A few days later a letter arrived from his solicitors accusing me of abuse and asking for monetary contributions and threatening of eviction. I decided to discuss it with Mr X and tell him I would like my furniture from his sister and we would leave. He told me not be silly and he would speak to his solicitors. I knew he was playing with me. I said nothing to my sons, I am not sure why, maybe embarrassment or out of shame.

I rang his sister and told her I would like to make arrangements to collect my furniture but she hung up the phone on me. I knew then I might never retrieve my furniture.

Chapter 9
I will destroy you!

The atmosphere in the house had become extremely tense in the last month. I felt restless. Mr X tried in vain to be nicer, after he realised that boundary lines were being re-established, but realising my mind was made up and I wanted out, he once again flipped the script and became even more ruthless. Solicitor's letters would arrive frequently. He started locking parts of the house to restrict movement and openly told me what I had to do if I wanted to stay there. I threatened to go to the police and tell them about my past experiences and my furniture and that seemed to calm him down for a few days but I never let my guard down and I knew he was scheming and planning behind the scenes.

One evening Mr X grabbed me around my waist and I told him no!

'Know this,' he breathed into my face, 'if you ever go to the Police, I will spend every last cent dragging you through the courts and ruin you financially. I will not stop, I will destroy you! I will fight you and take Son 3 away. Mark my words!' And for the first time I saw in his eyes that he was deadly serious, and inside I shivered. I had looked deep into the heart of evil and I was scared.

Months later his threats became real. In courts he would lie explicitly and appeared the picture of propriety. It somehow seemed he could cast his spell on everyone. With the aid of family members he diagnosed me as mentally ill and I had to subject myself to questions from an officer appointed by the courts to assess my sanity.

I managed a feeble, 'whatever! Do what you want. I'm not scared of you,' but I knew I was. I unconsciously stepped back and lowered my eyes which was a sure sign that I had given him the upper hand. He recognised this and smirked. I turned and walked away but I could feel his icy stare on the back of my neck, I quickened my steps to disappear around the corner and bolted for the outside. I stood there for a while just leaning against the wall staring blindly and could feel the tears in my eyes but I would not cry and so I forced them back.

*****

I did not see or smell him, but somehow I could sense his malevolent presence before he appeared around the corner. 'Are you going to tidy up that utility room?' he barked. 'You have clothes sitting there for days,' he growled. I nodded and smiled. I did not want to smile but his threats still sounded in my ear and I was scared. Mom, my sister and children were upstairs and I did not want them to hear so I dejectedly walked towards the utility room. He followed behind me closely. A single tear escaped and I quickly wiped it away. 'You're not going to speak tonight, are you?' he sneered.

I had to go tonight but I did not know what to say. I didn't want to upset Mr X even more.

'Not really, I just needed to drop off their box. I didn't even remember I had it in my boot,' I replied with feigned irritation. I bent to take up the clothes basket with my back to him because I did not want to see him. He immediately stepped up behind me and as I stood up his arms encircled my waist with his right hand creeping up to cup my breast.

I froze and felt sickened to my heart. My skin felt dirty as if my mind wanted to run away and leave my body there.

He leaned over my shoulder and I could smell his sweet breath near my ear. 'You're sleeping in my room tonight!' he commanded. I swallowed hard. 'Do you hear me?'

'Yes,' I answered, my voice sounding strained. Another tear escaped.

'The door is still open,' I whispered keeping my voice at a steady tone.

'Vin!' My mother's voice came from the kitchen. Rescue had arrived.

'I'm here Mom!' I responded quickly, a little bit too quickly because Mr X's brow furrowed. I opened the door and I started talking trying to overcompensate. 'Mr X was just helping me fold laundry,' I laughed erratically. 'He's so helpful sometimes,' I smiled. 'Hon, are you eating before I go or are you waiting up for me?' I asked, praying he would opt for the former. No such luck.

'I'm waiting for you, darling.' He leaned over for a kiss and I kissed him. I glanced at Mom but she didn't look convinced so once again I started to overcompensate by chatting non-stop about random things, sharing humorous stories about Mr X and silly mundane stories about him and every so often I would laugh and even manage to pat his arms in the process.

Mr X excused himself and I smiled at mom and moved

quickly with the basket upstairs so she would not ask.

*****

Another letter arrived as I sat down to eat my breakfast later the following week. I had not told anyone about the letters. Mr X had met the mailman outside and collected the day's post. He walked into the kitchen with a kind of strange smirk on his face. I tried to decipher what it meant but drew a blank.

'Just having breakfast?' he enquired.

'Yes, I went to bed late last night,' I replied looking him straight in the eye. Lately sometimes I would find a hidden and unexpected strength to be bold and stand up for myself but always mindful not to anger him too much. My strength never lasted very long but I was comforted to know it was there beneath the ashes, a smouldering ember eager to be reignited and consume the weakened and hopeless person I had somehow become. One day I thought to myself, one day soon this will all be over . . . but when? I could not see the metaphorical light at the end of the tunnel, only pitch black, but I believed that someday I would find a light even it I had to fan my inner flame to guide me out of the darkness.

He stood looking at me as I slowly ate my porridge waiting and I did not look up to meet his gaze. After an interminably long time he chuckled and threw a letter in front of me. 'The mail came,' he snorted then moved to the kettle to make his morning coffee. I continued eating my porridge.

The whistle of the kettle made me flinch, dragging me

back from imaginary sojourn. I did that a lot then; I would be seated next to someone but my mind ran as if to escape me and my physical surroundings. Today I was riding on a tractor full of hay. I kept pulling little bits of hay from my hair and chucking it at the dark gentleman seated on the next bale. Somehow he appeared in most of my imaginative journeys, a knight in shining armour.

'Well?' he croaked as he sat down. 'Aren't you going to open it?' He indicated the letter he had thrown in front of me.

'No thank you!' I replied, 'from your expression I know whatever is inside will cause me pain and today, just for today, I chose to be happy.' He glared at me but did not say one more word. I got up, scraped the uneaten porridge into a plastic bag and place it carefully into one of the three bins we had been instructed to use.

He moved to the dining table and I wished I could have another route of escape but the kitchen door remained firmly blocked with a box on the other side to prevent anyone using that exit. I washed my plate very very slowly delaying the journey to go past him. When the plate had been cleaned about ten times, I dried it and placed it in the cupboard, wiped up any water that might have dropped onto the floor or the kitchen counter, and placed the towel back in its exact position. I then checked the porridge and milk were in the exact place I found them. I then took a deep breath as if I was about to jump off a high bridge and quickened my steps to pass him as quickly as I could.

He was waiting. As I attempted to go past he grabbed my

arm in a forceful grip. I tried to make light of the situation and he chuckled. 'You left your letter on the table.'

'I know, but I will get it later,' I replied.

'Take it up now,' he commanded. I swallowed hard then turned to go back but he was still gripping my arm which restricted my movements. I said nothing but stood there my body half twisted towards the kitchen table in my attempt to retrieve this letter.

He slowly stood up, because he wanted to be more menacing. I knew he was in constant pain but not as severe as I wished it to be. He stood and pulled me back on to him and reached his other hand around my body. I turned away quickly to escape his sickening touch but ended up face to face with him. He smiled. Feeling his hand tighten and realising he was stronger I resorted to coyness and humour.

I smiled and bent at the waist to break that close contact. 'The neighbours Mr X,' I said. He looked around and his grip loosened a bit. As soon I felt the temporary easing of his grip I quickly pulled away escaping his grasp and rushed to the other end of the kitchen. I picked up the letter. As if on cue, by luck or mercy, his phone rang. He leaned over to retrieve it from his coat hanging from the back of his chair. With lightning speed I went past him, into the boys' lounge and straight up the stairs.

'Are you ok mom?' Son 1 peeked his head outside his room.

'Yes baby, I'm okay, love. Are you getting up now my little sleepyhead?'

'Mom I've been up since 7 am and already went for a

walk.'

'How many steps?'

'Ten thousand,' he replied.

'Well done my baby"

'Can we please go out today mom?' he asked. I knew that 'please' was not because he was polite even though he was. That 'please' meant I needed an escape from my prison.

'Of course. Let me wake your brothers up and then we can go .' His smile would have lit up Wembley stadium.

I went inside the toilet and read the letter. It was from his solicitor telling me I needed to now contribute £1,000.00 per month and outlining that I had been violent to him. I knew somehow he did not tell anyone *why I* had been violent to him. Solicitor letters became a regular fixture in my life from that point and after each letter he would become a bit more intolerable and a bit more demanding. I suffered in silence with the ever present smile, waiting until I had enough money to escape.

*****

By April, we had settled into a routine. I did not even feel anything anymore. I was just an empty, smiling shell of myself. My only solace was writing and speaking.

One morning, by the time I had packed my bed away and glanced through the windows his car was gone. I cannot describe to you the feeling of jubilation that swept through my body. It was as if one had been released prematurely from a life sentence, it was unbridled joy. I went out to the landing and started with my air guitar singing, 'Don't put the blame on me,' and was in my full performance singing when the bedroom doors burst open one by one because everyone knew he was gone. All three boys were back-up singers in their pyjamas, Mom was on drums and my sister Debbie on keyboards. We rocked that song for fifteen minutes and laughed and laughed and laughed.

The doors were left ajar, we spoke loud enough for everyone to hear, we were free and uninhibited. We felt alive. We did not speak, we felt. No words were spoken but eyes told the full story. We embraced tightly. Soon.

*****

I did not have any close girlfriends that I could speak to about these issues so I took refuge in my writing. I wrote poems and I started writing my journal. I wrote my journal at nights hidden away or parked in my car somewhere remote. I chose these locations not only for quiet isolation but more for privacy. No one would believe me and the questions that would follow scared me. I also wrote in code just in case my journal was ever lost or invaded by prying eyes. But my poems were different. I wrote those everywhere. I wrote on my mobile phone, on scraps of paper and in books. The more pain I felt, the more the words flowed; it was my spring of creativity and I harnessed my anger and used it to fuel my writing and managed to write fifty poems in seven days. I loved writing poetry, a talent I never knew I had, because I embraced the freedom of poetic license it gave me. I shared with a few friends sometimes and was pleased with the responses. The words didn't have to be about me and even when asked about the dark poems I had written, I repeatedly denied that they were. To create even more confusion, I started mixing my serious poetry with funny and silly poems that had just surface meanings. It lessened the interrogations and I was left in peace.

Writing

Writing is my truth
Writing is my peace
Writing is my salvation

Writing grounds me to earth
Writing give me increase
Writing is my meditation

Writing takes my youth
Writing give me sweet release
Writing is my education

Writing is my truth
Writing gives me peace
Writing is my salvation

The tone of my poems started changing in early 2017 when I had some positive inspiration from a most unlikely source - a distant friend, distant in memories, distant in friendship and distant in geographical location - but somehow his voice and our random discussions calmed me from the inside and I tapped into this source to give me a bit of balance in my crazy upside-down world. It was like morphine to someone in pain, like a drop of water to someone lost in the desert and I craved his friendship but I said nothing. It was not about love or any type of relationship with him and although we flirted a bit there was no plan or intention to take it any further. He was just a voice in the mist that comforted and inspired me.

My emotional crutch though he never suspected it. I had mentally decided that love was never going to be a part of my future. I was done.

Chapter 10
Self discovery

I know

I still know what you did to me
Even though the world may not see
A story well constructed,
Lies cleverly orchestrated,
Though the facts may not be clear
My story remains authentic and sincere
I did what I had to do and allowed you into my bed
Just to keep a roof over my children's head

You changed my life from what it used to be
Physically and emotionally abused me until I had to flee
You tried to break my soul
With words and actions not yet told
My bed you defiled
To destroy my inner child
I struggle painfully through each night
Trusting that everything will work out alright
While you walk about feeling like you're the man
I struggle to regain who I am.

For the pain my children went through
All because of you
Your conscience will never be free
Until you make amends for the hurt you caused me
I won't allow you to write my story's end
It will be written by me, by my hand and by my pen.

One day I stopped. Not mentally or in my imagination but physically stopped as I was walking to my, car causing those following too close to bump into my back. A few people apologised, some directed looks of irritation while others were more vocal in their disagreement with my sudden halt that momentarily shaved a few microseconds off their time to get to wherever they were going.

It all unfolded in slow motion around me and made no impact on me physically or emotionally. 'How did I get here?' I questioned myself, actually whispering out aloud. I seemed to have walked inside my body up to my brain, opened the door and demanded the answer. In a mad bid to get an answer, my brain quickly scanned over recent events and the fleeting imagery made my eyes well up with tears, my shoulders moved up and down and slow sobs escaped my mouth.

I felt like I was breaking once again. The realisation that I was stood in the middle of the footpath leading to the car park crying suddenly became apparent and I hastily dried my eyes, adjusted my clothes, wiped my eyes then headed to my car. I knew with 100% certainty exactly what I needed to do right then. I walked with urgency and the fixed intent of a person who had discovered their purpose. I no longer cared what people might think or what they might say. I had to leave. I had to get out. We were being abused.

I am her

I am woman
I will not be broken
Too long I have been used and abused.
Treat me like property
Rented and tokened
Head bowed and lips pursed
Here it is preached that silence is golden
No freedom…
Walk where we are instructed
Spirits beholden
Too much to cry
Soul awakens
I break free
The world is mine
Spirit unshaken
I soar above
My bonds are finally broken.

It was always the nights that were the hardest for me, simply because I was alone with my thoughts and the darkness hid my tears and my fears It was in the darkness I cried out because the pain inside became almost unbearable and in the dark I no longer needed to be strong. In the dark I was alone and there was no one to judge me.

But then I also sometimes got scared of the dark, I must confess. It scared me because it was harder to control my thoughts and the dark thoughts crept into my mind and threatened to take over. Each time I ventured too close to that edge between dark and light I thought about my children and saw them standing in the light calling to me and waiting there for me, so I walked back from the strong allure of the forgetfulness and an end to all of my problems promised by the dark. That night I fought against the call of the abyss and started to read my Bible in earnest. I dared not turn on the light to attract attention or reprimand. I read using my phone light and found peace but still sleep eluded me.

Elusive Rest

Sleep, sweet sleep why elude my tired eyes
I beg you come and provide my escape
I toss and turn and my mind wander
I see devils and demons in the same repeated shape

Capturing my thoughts and wrestling in my mind
He stalks my every waking hour
He is always near plotting and scheming
I need to escape his over-reaching power

Sleep, sweet sleep come and give me just a short rest
Closing my eyes so I can quietly forget
Wrap me in your blissful unconscious state
Please, come and rescue Vinette

*****

After Mom had come to stay with me, the pain had subsided for a while. Mr X was a bit nicer when she came initially but after just a few weeks he had started again. I felt Mom could sense something was wrong but I never told her anything. He was always careful not to do anything when she was around or within earshot and this gave me some well needed respite.

Because she was around I got a little bit more leverage to continue my speaking without the usual worry about the children or the constant scrutiny and checking of my phone. The first time I caught him on my phone he pretended he was examining the case but then as time passed he became a bit more brazen and on more than one occasion I had to show messages to prove where I was, what I was doing and where I was going. I did it just to maintain the peace.

Speaking eased my pain and gave me a welcomed distraction. I enjoyed writing speeches and delivering them.

Chapter 11
And the winner is. . .

I sat on the edge of my seat holding on to the hand of my good friend M. The contest chair had already announced third and second place . . . only first place was left and like any good MC, she dragged out this pause for what seemed like an interminably long time.

I held my breath, I am sure I had stopped breathing ten minutes before.

This win meant more. It was not the trophy or the congratulations but the self-validation and the hope that it brought to my life. Pure and simple, hope, hope to leave my situation and make a better life for my children, hope to start writing my own story once again, hope to save myself. Speaking and the family it brought with it was keeping me going and no one even realised it. Toastmasters was keeping me going, giving me hope and providing a platform for me to dream. I had found my purpose.

The last remaining glass trophy stood there waiting for the worthy recipient. I wanted to hear my name so badly, I was screaming inside my head.

'And the winner is ... drum roll please ... Vinette Hoffman-Jackson.'

I heard it but now I did not believe it, could not believe it. I had hoped, prayed, dreamt and wished for it but I was expecting fate's cruel hand to snatch it way at the last moment.

I looked at M, and whispered, 'did they call my name?'

Before he could answer, his huge grin told me they had. I saw hands go together, people looking at me, huge smiles as I walked from the back of the room to the stage.

I kept praying that I would not start crying or stumble over my words. The joy I felt was indescribable. The future suddenly looked a lot brighter. A ray of hope. I walked quickly to the stage to collect my ticket to deliverance.

I stood there and quickly reflected on my journey through the Toastmasters speaking competition, from club to area to division and finally I was at district and I had won.

I know everyone enters a competition to win but sometimes the stories behind the individuals add another dimension. I felt like *somebody* once again. It was the start of something new and exciting. However, later as I drove back home, my elation gave way to a deep sense of foreboding yet again. This would be difficult to keep as a secret. Even though the competition had progressed through the different rounds and I had won all the rounds, whereas most people would proudly show off their trophies, mine was just a quick pic on Facebook then taken down and locked in my car boot to keep the peace. I had made the mistake of sharing after my very first win.

After my first win, life had start to become even more unbearable. I did not clean something well enough or I missed something off the supermarket list. Post-its to remind me of my many failures would be scattered all over the house. I took it all in stride. I wanted to focus on the bigger prize, the world championship of public speaking.

I drove home that Sunday afternoon in May fully thinking maybe I should keep my win a secret but as soon as I entered the drive and realised the black hearse was not in the drive, joy overcame me and I rushed inside to share my achievement with my family. My mom screamed, my sons and sister were laughing and hugging me. I forgot everything and cried with joy. We were so caught up in the moment that we did not hear the bogey mobile parking on the drive nor the front door opening either nor the footsteps coming towards us.

People have always told me I had a presence but this was different. As if on cue everyone froze without even seeing him, we knew he was there. All the joy disappeared and everyone felt the chill. He looked at us in our semi-frozen state, looked at the trophies and did not say one word.

He walked outside and we shuffled away but I knew: I felt that something major was about to happen. In the next few days he did not touch me and the only person he spoke with was Mom and his son. Then letters started arriving from his solicitors with demands for money and asking us to leave his property.

I rang his sister: no answer. I emailed her to ask if we could arrange a time to collect my furniture: no answer. I visited her home and knocked at the door, but no one answered. I told Mr X, I would be leaving but I needed my furniture; he smirked then told me I would need to travel to his country of origin to get most of it back. I did not speak. I was determined to sleep on the floor if I had to but the Lord sometimes works in mysterious ways. I started packing and informed everyone we would be leaving after Son 1 finished his exams.

After dinner one evening when everyone was in bed, a deep sense of dread overshadowed me and my heart started racing uncontrollably. I heard the creaking of floorboards upstairs. I grabbed some papers pretending I was about to mark and waited. I sat with papers perched on my lap and marking pen on hand. Footsteps on the stairs startled me and I jumped resulting in all the papers falling to the floor. I quickly jumped up, panic in my movements as the door to the second reception open ended I looked up a wave of relief washed over me. It was just Son 1. 'Are you ok mom? You look a bit stressed.'

'Yeah I'm fine hon! Just catching up on my marking.'

'Can you … follow me to the kitchen?' The second half of his statement was a mere whisper. He gestured toward the upstairs and I knew that he was scared to go into the kitchen just in case Mr X came downstairs but I said nothing, It was just another reminder that I needed to move.

*****

My final day in that house started like any other day. It was totally unplanned. I had wanted to wait until my son had finished his A-Levels and move in the summer holidays. Mr X had become ever more intolerable and I had managed to escape his advances for over a month and this frustrated him and so he told me to leave his house. I had convinced him that I would leave Son 3 with him if he allowed Son 1 to finish his exams and miraculously he agreed. It was my only option.

I was on my best behaviour during that time, anxious not to upset Mr X. If I violated a rule, I quickly apologised and corrected my error. I made sure the house was cleaned daily. I limited my visits to Toastmasters. I cooked, I smiled, I ironed, I smiled, I helped in the garden, I smiled.

I had saved up £4,000.00.

I was pretending to be asleep in my sons' room one afternoon when I was suddenly awakened by Mr X shaking my back. He had returned home unexpectedly. I slowly opened my eyes to see his dark looming figure. 'I would like to talk to you,' he said. I shivered and suddenly became scared. Why did he walk in while everyone was happy? I remained stationary for a while trying to gather my thoughts and plan a few lies just in case someone was caught out by his return.

I steadied my nerves then walked slowly as if I was going to the gallows. I knocked lightly at his bedroom door. 'Come in,' he thundered. I tentatively opened the door and walked in. He stood with his side to me folding laundry.

'Yes,' I said.

'I need to talk to you,' he repeated. I stepped closer but remained within reach of the door. He placed the large towel he had just finished folding on top of the pile, causing the entire pile to start toppling. Instinctively I reached out my hands to catch it before it felt to the floor but completely missed the pile so it fell to the floor. Without thought I stepped closer to collect the fallen items and in one swift movement he caught my arms as I stood up and pushed me onto the bed. My eyes opened wide as he pinned my arms and used his knees to try and push open my legs, his hands started lifting my dress. My eyes opened wide at the realisation at what was about to happen with my children, mother and sister in the house and all were awake. In blind panic I somehow got enough strength; I hooked my foot under the *chaise longue* to gain leverage and manage to push him off me then ran to the open door and fled downstairs, breathing heavily.

I reached the lounge, sat down and grabbed my laptop pretending to work. Two minutes later he walked through the door and sat next to me. He put his hands to touch me. 'Stop!' I screamed but in a hushed tone. He reached out again and I quickly got up to get away. He reached out to grab my arm and caught my dress, ripping the shoulder straps, tied together where they had previously broken.

Up until that moment I did not realise that Son 3 was in the room. 'Daddy!' he yelled, 'why did you rip Mom's dress?' I was suddenly overcome by the shock realisation that my son had witnessed this event. A few seconds later the door opened and my sister walked into the room closely followed by my mom.

'Vin are you ok?' my sister asked. Embarrassment, confusion and fears all melted into one and I felt like my head and heart was about to explode. Every rational thought escaped my mind and it felt like the world was moving in slow motion. I was talking, screaming, crying but I had no idea if I was even making sense. I grabbed Son 3 into my arms and yelled to Mr X, 'I'm going to the police!'

'You are the one they will arrest' he shouted after me but his voice crackled nervously.

I smelled fear. 'Let them,' I responded. I had finally had enough, a cell would have been refuge away from him.

*****

I rushed past Mom and my sister without a word. I did not want to speak to anyone at home. 'Look after Sons 1 and 2,' I shouted behind me. I quickly strapped Son 3 into my car and sped away before anyone could convince me to stay. I did not really know where the police station was and so I drove around twice and then made up my mind to speak with his brother-in-law who seemed to have the most sense in that family, so I headed towards his house. I cannot tell you if I passed six cars or twelve or how many stop lights were on green. I drove as if I was in a trance and got there in a zombie-like state.

I parked haphazardly, grabbed our son from the backseat and rushed to the front door of his sister-in-law and pounded on the door. No answer came but I kept up my unrelenting assault with my fist. When no answer came, the realisation that they might not be home suddenly became clear. With our son perched on my hips I leaned against the door and started sobbing.

'Mommy, mommy don't cry,' our son pleaded and used his little hands to wipe away my tears. I walked back to my car and just sat. What on earth was I going to do? I knew I could never go back but what could I do? I looked over at our son and realised that for his sake and for the sake of my other children I had to put a stop to this. The tears started again and I dialled 999. I knew there was no coming back. 'Hello, 999. . . . . '

*****

Mr X was arrested that night and spent the night in jail. For the first time in months that night I felt safe and slept soundly.

In a hotel room at the local Premier Inn I cried, not because of all I had been through but because of what I had put my children through. I cried and promised myself, it would never happen again.

The three boys were in an adjoining room and I shared my room with my sister and mother. I walked into my sons' room to console them as I figured they would be in floods of tears and distraught, instead they rushed into my arms with the largest smiles possible. 'Mom we're free!' Son 2 shouted. I had not heard his real voice in months; I could not believe their joy. They had just moved from a five-bedroom home to a hotel room but they were happy and carefree.

Children are resilient. Quite often we make decisions thinking it is best for them but the truth is they can survive anywhere they feel loved, safe and protected. Material things are just a bonus. We spent over a week in the hotel and it was fast eating into our cash reserve so I approached the local council for help. We were given emergency accommodation within the next two days.

We were allowed by the police to go back to the property and collect stuff and there and then I decided to take beds, tables and items I would need to furnish my new accommodation. Mr X reported theft to the police who came while I was moving. I explained that he and his sister had all my belongings and the police did nothing to stop me from taking the beds and the few items I needed. I placed the things I managed to take in a local storage facility.

Even though Mr X and his sister had all my furniture he still reported me to the police and started sending me letters from his solicitors demanding the return of his property. However he has still not pursued a claim YET through the civil court - although I have been repeatedly threatened about it. As this book is going to print I have still not exchanged furniture with his sister. In late August 2018, he had after locked my furniture and belongings away for two years and refused to return them, I got an email that he was ready to exchange the items. I did not respond.

*****

D drive. That's a full sentence in itself. It was emergency accommodation, no frills just the basics amenities. I looked around with a plastic smile pasted across my face. The gentleman doing the paperwork was very kind. 'First time?' he asked.

'Yeah ! First and last,' I replied. I looked away.

I hurriedly signed the documents he presented, collected the keys and left the house. I drove in silence to the hotel. No radio or cd, nothing. 'Got somewhere, I announced on entry to the hotel room.' 'It is not home but it will have to do for a while.' No one moved.

*****

When I was young, my grandmother would always break bad news to us in a special way. She would take whatever news she had and make it seem ten times worse and when we were sufficiently depressed she would give us the bad news but by then it would seem like it was good news compared to the prior alternative. I decided to try this technique.

'Well remember it is temporary so people are in and out daily. Some may be drug dealers, or refugees or abuse victims so it is basically grab and go. The houses is old and to be honest (It was not) there may be rats.' My sons look horrified and momentarily I felt awful.

We had no beds so we had to wait a day to get some delivered. I was petrified they might have had second-hand used mattresses but we were lucky to receive brand new beds and I was grateful. I spent the first day with Mom, bleaching and cleaning everything in sight, from toilets to light switches. I made numerous trips to the storage facility to collect the items we needed and we tried to settle in as best we could because my sons still had school to attend.

I was petrified each morning I dropped off Son 3 that he would be taken by Mr X but surprisingly Mr X never showed up to visit him at school ,except at sports day in late July. He later filed for full custody and it then became clear why no attempts were ever made to see his son. He told the courts that he was kept away from his son and did not know where his son was for over three months even though his son's school was within a mile of his home. Despite this, I texted his niece to arrange visits but was ignored. It would give his case more credibility if it appeared that I was preventing parental contact.

After a week in D drive, we were informed that once again we had to move to temporary accommodations. We were once again packing to move.

Chapter 12
The storage unit

I was sat flat on the floor in the middle of open boxes, their contents strewn all over the floor. I sat there for a few minutes staring at the stack of boxes, pieces of furniture and the odd piece of clothes sticking out of suitcases that were hurriedly packed without any care or pride.

I felt the pain in my lower back but it was relegated to the back of my mind as my emotions took centre stage and my memory went racing back yet again to my life in the previous few months. I didn't move; I just sat there for a while.

Then I felt it. That feeling when you suddenly realise you're not alone. I slowly turned my head to see my company. It was the manager of the storage depot. He looked at me quizzically then, when he had pieced together the series of events that must have occurred prior to his arrival, he surmised I had tried to climb on items in the unit and had fallen over. He quickly walked towards me and asked, 'are you okay?' He stretched an arm out to offer his help. The full picture was not apparent until he walked up to me and looked into the storage unit and saw the trail of devastation left by my man-made avalanche. Immediately I could see the H&S bells ticking and his solicitor's defence being planned. 'Did you fall?' he asked with uncertainty, allowing the end of his voice to rise as if to gently coax the answer he required.

'No!' I replied with sarcasm, 'I just thought I would sit

in the middle of a self-storage unit on my bum watching boxes.' That was followed by an eye squint and folded lips as if a dare. He saw my dare and decided it would be prudent not to proceed.

His tone immediately softened. 'Do you need some help?' he asked.

I smiled. 'No, I'm good,' I replied, getting to my feet. 'I'm okay.' I didn't look in his direction but started to busy myself repacking the boxes. I then went back inside storage unit Number 1 to tidy up the aftermath of my avalanche.

The storage unit was a daily visit for me. Everything was kept there in that warehouse, everything I had left in the material world. Today I needed some pots and some clothing for my children. I started arranging stuff once again, making sure I did not climb on anything and fall a second time. After about fifteen minutes I found a box with pots but no lids. Cooking would have to be fine without lids tonight. I pulled out two saucepans and two plates from a neighbouring box that caught my eye. Still no sign of the clothing or shoes that I needed.

I gathered my pots and plates then, placing them on the ground outside, pulled down the door to my storage unit Number 1. I then recollected my pots and plates and headed over to storage unit Number 2. I set my stash down on the floor once again then opened the door. This was the bigger of the two units and in our haste we had not had time to organise everything in order. It looked like a landfill site and I stood there looking for a moment unsure of where to start. From the left corner the manager appeared and flippantly started checking the units next to me. Somehow I think he was there just to ensure that I did not have another accident. I ignored him. He tried to make small talk but I still ignored him.

I tentatively stepped inside fearful the whole thing might topple over on top of me. There was a sofa base to the right and on top was an upturned night table; several black bin-liners were skilfully balanced on top. On top of the bin-liners, half of a suitcase was perched precariously on top the other half, supported by a dining chair that was leaning dangerously to the right but prevented from falling by boxes with some unknown contents that were themselves supported by another dining chair. The boxes were about five to six deep and stacked to the ceiling in a haphazard fashion and I couldn't help drawing some parallel to my life at that very moment. I smiled at the analogy.

Cautiously I opened a suitcase that was on the floor to the right of the unit and all the clothes I was looking for were in that one suitcase at the front of the door. Although this might seem a simple and random act it was enough to cause tears to well up in my eyes. In those times, the little things meant so very much and I literally looked up and whispered a grateful 'thank you'; someone, somewhere was still looking out for me. I pulled the case clear of the door then pulled it down and locked it. I dragged the suitcase with one hand and balanced my pots and plates in the other and headed for my car. It was 3 pm.

*****

The guys at the storage unit got to know me really well

after two weeks and we occasionally exchanged pleasantries on my daily runs, which were now two to three per day. We discussed just general things like the weather and any current news item but they never once asked further and I was grateful for that. My story had been locked inside and I protected it. I was a mother protecting her young. No one must ever know. The thought of people knowing what I was going through scared and embarrassed me equally.

I was also overprotective of my children; I did not want their names in the system. I looked for every and any change in their actions, moods or words, anything to make sure they were coping. I overcompensated and they were allowed to eat whatever they liked to eat: ice-cream at 9pm on a Monday night, done; too tired for homework, done; television until late, done. These were my offers to my children. They could do whatever they liked but they never took up any of my offers. An occasional request for sweets which I happily obliged, or a trip to the park which I joyfully facilitated. At that point I would have done anything to distract them and make them happy.

As it turned out, the material things or the lack of television or the reduced income did not really matter. In fact I dare to say they were far happier than when they were living in a half-million-pound house. There was a joy and happiness and a sense of identity in their eyes that had been absent for months. They spoke with confidence, stood straight and articulated their opinions without fear. They opened and closed doors as they pleased and sat whenever they wanted, wherever they wanted and however they wanted.

Cuddles and kisses were constantly showered on me and I embraced everyone with the biggest smile. I realised then that life is all about love, unconditional and boundless love. My smiles started to grow bigger each day.

Chapter 13
V Street

Alone

I'm a ghost, invisible, unseen
A figment of your imagination
I'm here but never ever seen
A fleeting apparition
Searching searching everywhere I go
But it is always night and I'm but a shadow
An occasional smile, simple reflex
Not defined by the existing context
To be polite
A mere acknowledgement on sight
I speak but it is like wind, a wisp of air
My opinion disappear into the atmosphere
I have no value, I am mist
Casually dismissed

Can you not feel my loneliness
I am here! I'm here ! feeling depressed
Searching for a friendly face
Someone, anyone please I'm not just empty space

If D drive was a sentence then V street was the full chapter.

The house reeked and not the type of smell that bleach and air freshener could shift. The smell seemed to be built into the walls and would not go away. The lady checking me in looked me over and immediately realised I did not belong there. This place was even more basic than before with no beds. 'What will we sleep on?' I naively enquired.

Her face registered that her suspicions were confirmed: I did not belong there. 'I'm sorry but we don't provide beds. There's a second hand shop but…' The horrified look on my face told her she had gone up the wrong path with that suggestion. She recovered quickly by adding '… but I don't suppose you'll want that.' I shook my head to show she had arrived at the right conclusion.

I thanked her and collected the keys. I stood alone in that house and cried. Little gentle sobs at first then huge torrents that shook my entire body. I cried until no sound came and the back of my heart felt like it was about to split open. I was once again in the depths of despair.

After a few minutes I realised I needed to once again be strong for my children. My moment was over. A knock on the door dragged my feet back to earth suddenly. I peeked through the window to see an old man standing there. It was a new neighbourhood and I was alone so I cracked the window in the lounge. 'Hello.'

'Hey, sorry to bother you but you're parked in front of my gate. Could you move your car?' he said quite politely.

'I'm sorry! I'll move it now.' I hastily grabbed my keys and went out. I did not want to upset anyone in the neighbourhood. He stood outside waiting, his car stopped in the middle of the road.

'Nice car,' he said with that same puzzled look I had seen before. That look that says, what are you doing here? And I could usually see the person writing their own story about my life. I said nothing, just a nod and that smile.

I reversed up the street, found a tight parking spot and squeezed in. I grabbed my ever present cleaning materials from the boot and went back inside to start my cleaning. I had high hopes of eradicating that smell. I would bleach everything in sight.

I glanced back to make sure my car was locked and immediately a feeling of gratitude consumed me. I started listing all the things I was grateful for, starting with my life and my health. I started my affirmations, telling myself this is only for a season but my reward shall come and went back to dreaming about that lovely six-bedroom house out in Oxfordshire on three acres of land with a little stream running at the back. I walked through each room cleaning anything and everything and singing on top of my voice. I was jolted back to reality with Whitney Houston and a high note in her song, one moment in time. I coughed, held my throat and smiled.

Three bottles of bleach later I knew everything was sterilised including door handles and every cupboard in the house. I rang Mom because we needed beds. A mother will always be a mother forever. I was once again grateful for my mother being there. She had her own lovely home in Jamaica but chose to stay with me during my homelessness and I was so grateful to her. I was truly blessed. The important things in life had not shifted, they were firmly rooted to help guide me through those dark days.

Mom started working the phones to find cheap moving vans who could act on quick notice. Three hours later we found one and rushed to the storage unit to retrieve the beds we had taken. By 8 pm we had all the basics in place.

Son 1 with his Asperger had hypersensitive smell sensitivity and the smell in the house drove him crazy. He took refuge at the nearby Subway and would stay there for hours studying for his A levels. I was petrified he would be asked to leave but the staff were very pleasant and since he was well behaved they allowed him to sit quietly in one corner and study. Even this simple act made me grateful.

I sat with him sometimes to make light of the situation. I explained how much we still had to be grateful to God for. I knew this was one moment in his life that would help create his reference line. For me reference lines are those moments, events or decisions that act as turning points in one's life. They become the point of reference for future and past events. We refer to them and say 'three months after…' or 'a few weeks before…' We would compare occurrences to that reference point. 'If you think this is bad then… or this is a step up from…. V Street, which would be one such reference point.

*****

After my hotel sojourn, and after buying food from restaurants and cafés, or for petrol to drive around to find accommodations and for storage fees, my savings were dwindling fast. I had to get some additional income which meant more stress on an already highly tense situation. Then I remembered that I had signed up to mark examination scripts. There is always one light left on so you can find your way out of the darkness.

I quickly called in to explain that I needed to mark and apologised for being late. Luckily for me they still had space and readily accepted me. I was allocated five hundred scripts, which seemed like a mountain to mark in that short frame of time with no permanent abode amongst so many other issues. Believing and trusting that a way would be found, I accepted the contract. I bought a portable device to access the internet then I started. Through the nights when everyone was sleeping, I marked; when the kids went to school, I marked; between meals, I marked. Sleep was now a privilege and not a right. I had made sure everyone had a bed and slept upstairs in a bedroom whilst I slept on single blown-up mattress on the floor downstairs. It was uncomfortable and half-way through the night the air would escape and I would find myself on the cold hard wood floor. I would simply wake up and start pumping again. Throughout each night I had to pump at least four times so sleep was not very peaceful nor comfortable.

Each time I woke up I would pump then mark a few scripts. When I was a quarter way through, I was offered the opportunity to mark more scripts, about three hundred and I gladly said, yes. Sleep would need to wait. I started increasing my pace.

I would take three hours each day to hunt for houses. My sister would email me possibilities and I would ring and then visit. Most houses were either too small, too far from the boys' schools or just not up to standard but I kept trying. I knew I had to get some rest after falling asleep at a stoplight one afternoon coming from yet another house visit. Eventually with the help of a very helpful, patient and understanding estate agent I found a place in Kempston, a four-bedroom house. I didn't care that everything was not perfect. I had found a semi-permanent residence for my boys and Mom. I smiled.

That very night I had my Toastmasters meeting and I went and it was business as usual. By now I was not as frequent as I used to be but I managed to win the Best Evaluator ribbon which made me happy because it meant another little light in my tunnel. My inner peace was starting to be restored.

Peace

Peace that resonates
Validates
Encapsulates
And consolidates
That's the peace you give to me
Peace that radiates
Accommodates
And emancipates
That's the peace you show to me
Peace that stimulates
Fascinates
And motivates
That's the peace you make me feel
Peace that contemplates
Advocates
And orchestrates
That's the peace you cultivates

Tomorrow was a new day. I smiled then drifted off to sleep. My grandmother always said that to me before she passed away: 'evil does not last forever,' and up until last year I believed this to be true but not anymore. If it is true then time is extremely slow where I live.

Why does it always seem like those who do evil win and you are left out in the cold watching them back in their ill-gotten gains? Where is the justice in that? I think the injustice actually causes more damage and pain that the actual crime against the person. This is because you choose to believe that those in authority and support roles are there for you and when you find out that they cannot be in your corner then you crumble inside, and at that point in your life, if you're not strong enough, then suicide and other options seem likely.

When the lights go out sometimes all you have is laughter! Luckily for me, I knew where to find my light when darkness overtook me. I reached out for my mother, my rock and she stood firm so I could lean on her without fear that she would move. My mother supported me in every way possible way, spiritually, financially, emotionally, mentally and, most importantly, with great humour. She found ways to make me laugh and in a moment I was transported from my current condition to somewhere fun and peaceful.

Mom could always diffuse any situation with laughter. After lifting over fifty boxes one day I came home dog tired and could not even eat a bite. I instead fell asleep on my air mattress on the floor. Instead of pity my mom chose to remind me of the pounds I must have lost yesterday and assured me that my dinner the previous night had not been wasted as she had eaten it in the night just to make sure I didn't feel too bad. We looked at each other for a few seconds then burst out laughing.

On another occasion my mom saw two pigeons that frequented the backyard at D drive. She gently chided them and told them food was low inside so in the interest of their self -reservation her advice to them was to fly away. For the record, I do not and have never eaten any pigeon that has wandered into my yard, nor is it my intention to do so in the future. They may seem trivial but those moments were priceless and gave me the welcome breaks I needed.

Son 1 also stepped up like a man. I was the proudest mom. Even through he struggles with Asperger's and even though routines and changes were difficult for him, he never showed any signs of struggling to cope. His focus was on me and making sure I was okay. One of my favourite things in life was getting flowers. And even though funds were limited, one Saturday morning on his own intuition he walked to the nearest supermarket and came back with a bunch of yellow tulips and baby's breath. I was washing plates in the kitchen and had my back turned when he came up behind me and said, 'Mom, I love you, we will get over this!'

I turned to hug him and saw the flowers in his outstretched hands. Tears of joy rolled down my cheeks. I accepted my flowers in one hand and squeezed him in a tight hug with my other hand. That simple random act was enough fuel for me to get through the week ahead. If it was even possible, I loved him more than I ever did. He understood. He was my rock. I smiled.

I must admit that my faith at this point in my life suffered a knock. I did not give up on God but I felt abandoned and so I questioned the reasons. I asked the eternal question 'why me?' almost every night before the tears came and I drifted off to sleep. No answer came but slowly the days past and what seemed insurmountable withered into a distant memory and its power waned each day and the sadness became less and eventually manageable although there were frequent fluctuations in my temperament.

Emotions are a funny thing and sometimes the inner emotion is completely out of sync with the outward appearance. There were days when I felt sad, almost borderline depressed, but I walked a bit taller and smiled a bit wider, not to deceive the world but to force my inner emotions to sync with the outward appearance. I have also been told I looked angry when I was busy focussing and dreaming about something pleasant. The key I think is to get both inside and outside balanced to be a calmer and emotionally stronger person. An art I have tried on a regular basis since this experience. However, I remained faithful to my God and I was comforted by the story about Moses and the Red Sea. I believe he always turns up in our deepest darkest hour if we just have faith. He was my rock.

My final rock came from just hearing a distant voice that soothed me. Rodrigo would call, always at the perfect time, when I was nearing that breaking point and I reminded myself that my life was still a gift and I should always be grateful. Rodrigo was not an ardent Christian but he believed in the Creator and was constantly showing gratitude for everything. We would talk about music, life in Jamaica, future plans, jobs, children, politics and everything else under the sun. Time melted away when I spoke to him and everything for that moment in the world was right.

Birds were singing, flowers blooming, music was playing and there was world peace. It was beautiful and I smiled. He was my rock.

One of my favourite quotation is, 'I never lose, either I win or I learn.' Well, 2017 was certainly a year I would like to forget but I will always remember. It lifted me high and showed me what was possible by hard work and vision and it also brought me low and showed me pain and showed me the callousness of human beings. It gave me love but showed me what hatred means. I gave me happiness and showed me sadness. It made me a survivor and made me realise that, like bamboo, I bend but it takes more than that to break my spirit.

Chapter 14
The postman

Behind my smile

What do you do when you feel so lost
And want to be found at any cost
But no one ever seem to realise
And they look at you with unseeing eyes
When your eyes scream help me please
But your pain gets no immediate ease
Where do you go when you want to hide
from even those who stand by your side
When you just want a few hours of peace
Just for a moment to vent and release
When the noise around you get so loud
Away from the faceless crowd
Where do you go when you need to speak
When the pressure mounts week after week
When you feel like you have lost your voice
And you really have no choice
When all the things of this world you misunderstand
And you desperately try to figure out that distant plan
You simply smile and stretch forth your hand
God will calm your every emotion.

After about a month we finally moved to privately rented accommodation.

Then the letter came one day. It felt like someone had punched me in the stomach. I could literally feel my heart racing as I struggled to catch my breath. I did not open it; I just did not want to read the words. I somehow knew the content even before I opened and read it. The name of the solicitors were boldly printed on the front. I knew, whatever the contents, I was going to be in some sort of anguish. I ran upstairs and hid it under my bed. I just couldn't face it and its vitriol at that moment. I was busy trying to mentally prepare myself to compete in the finals of the public-speaking contest in Vancouver, Canada. The timing was so wrong and I felt it. I was tempted to cancel my trip to Canada but Mom insisted I go and do my best. Mentally I knew I was not prepared to deal with anything right then and the tears flowed everyday without warning. I felt like I was breaking which was my speech title. I smiled through my tears at the irony.

For the past few days I had been trying to get myself in the right state of mind and I had finally just about gotten there - and then that letter came. My usual smile was temporarily gone. Even though the letter was out of sight it was at the forefront of every thought, I could not shake it. It felt like a tonne of bricks pressing down on my shoulders and in fact my neck actually started hurting after a while.

The hours slowly passed and I delayed trudging upstairs to go to bed. I knew that letter was there waiting under my bed. I started to mentally rationalise. What was the worst that could happen? I could be ordered into court and my child taken away from me. What would I do? As a parent I think most times we fool ourselves into thinking our children need us most but I realised in that instance that I could not breathe without my children. I loved them more than my life itself and I would fight for them until my last breath.

I knew he had only filed for full custody to break me. He had threatened me repeatedly to bury me in court because he could afford to. No powers on earth could convince me that, miraculously, overnight, he wanted to be a full-time dad. This was a man who tried to bully me into an abortion and then when I would not, refused to sign a birth certificate, claiming this child was not his. Even when a DNA test was suggested, he flatly refused. He did not want to know. Despite this I travelled on many occasions over sixty miles to ensure my child had contact with his paternal relatives. After nearly a year he was finally convinced to accept parental responsibility but then promptly started another episode because he now refused to contribute to the support of his child. Finally I resorted to ask the Child Maintenance Agency to intervene but once again he had a plan for that too. Through clever accounting practices you can legally declare a minimal income in the form of a salary but withdraw dividends to fund your lifestyle which is what he did and ended up paying less than £16 per week, the same man who spent thousands of pounds with lawyers, yet a pittance on the upbringing of his son. I said nothing because I could not be bothered fighting anymore and he had disappeared from our son's life. This was the same man now after five years thought he was a better parent than me and wanted full custody and had the nerve to include in his suit that I could have extensive visits with my child. You could not make this up in an imaginary world yet there we were.

I showered and got into bed, closed my eyes and willed sleep to come but two hours later at 3 am I was still awake. I got out of bed and switched the lights on. I sat on the edge of the bed and could feel the envelope under my bed pulsating as if it was a living, breathing thing. When I could not resist any more I sat on the floor in front of my bed. I reached under my bed and gently took out the letter that I knew right there and then it would change my life forever. I took a deep breath and opened it.

I only needed to see the words 'court…' and the tears flowed. I cried silently, conscious that my other sons were asleep in the next room. As the tears stung my eyes, a huge painful lump was caught in my throat. What had I done to deserve this? I thought to myself.

I do not know when I fell asleep but I was awakened by a loud knock on my door. 'Vin, are you ok?' my mom asked.

I quickly got off the floor, and my entire body ached because I had fallen asleep in a somewhat awkward position on the floor. I banged my elbows on the metal side of the bed as I tried to regain my orientation. I hurriedly shoved all the papers back into the envelope and threw them under the bed again. I attempted to answer Mom but I could not find my voice, instead a hoarse voice replied, ' y y y es mom,

I am,' but I was not.

All moms I think are born with ESP. My mother could always sense when something was wrong but I could never bring myself to tell her everything. It would cause her pain and I did not see why both of us needed to suffer. That way she was protected and I would bear all the pain. It was my fault anyway, I thought.

The court date was two months away. I quickly filed the letter away mentally and refocussed on other priorities.

Vancouver came and went in a blur and before I knew it, it was time for my court appearance.

*****

I paced back and forth outside the courtroom like a caged animal, nervous, anxious and, if I was to admit, petrified; nervous because it was a court and I think everyone feels nervous even if you are completely innocent. It was just the uncertainty I suspect. Anxious because I was about to come face to face with the bogeyman and it made my heart beat erratically and my mouth felt dry. I was uncertain of my reactions and scared that I would once again start to break and I could feel the cracks appearing. I could not afford a solicitor and so I had to act on my own behalf which added another dimension to my already stressed mental state. I had spent hours each night reading up on the law and everything I could find.

I whispered a hollow prayer, because to be honest I felt a little bit abandoned by God. Why do good people always suffer? Finally, I hate to admit it but I felt scared because he was the monster that no one saw, like the bogey man under your bed. He was very clever and could weave his magic and, to the world looking in, he would appear to be the perfect gentleman. Mom held my hand to steady my shaking legs, turned and smiled to give me some quiet reassurance. I was so happy she was there with me.

'I did nothing wrong,' I whispered to Mom, 'did I?' I asked, uncertain of everything at that moment. Had I been a terrible mom because I refused Son 3's request for more sweets after he had already eaten a full pack? I had missed his school play because I had to work and he did have a scar on his leg when he fell over in the park. Should I have been watching him a bit more closely? Would they know and decide I was not a good mother? The questions kept jumping into my head and I felt weak.

'I'm sure someone will see that you're a good mom.' She patted my hands and we walked towards the door arm in arm. I was dressed in a grey tailored sleeveless dress with autumnal striped jacket and burgundy shoes with a black handbag and a rainbow striped bag with all my key notes. To complete the look a pair of Elle shades, not to protect the eyes from the sun but to hide the tears that burned at the corner of each eye. I looked the part of the solicitor and Mom, with anger emblazoned on her face, seemed to be the defendant. Despite my predicament I shared my thoughts with Mom and she managed a forced giggle. Her arm tightened and we marched through the big, heavy, brown, wooden door.

Its size betrayed its weight as it opened with just the slightest push and we walked in. Two security officers directed us to place our bags in trays then we walked through the metal detectors, naturally I beeped on my way through. I have always beeped at every airport security check I have ever been through. A seasoned veteran, I spread my arms in anticipation of the next step in the process. The officer smiled 'not necessary,' he mumbled, 'earrings!' Maybe he was fooled into thinking I was a solicitor, maybe but highly unlikely.

'Second floor,' he directed. We emptied our bags, re-attached our arms and marched up the stairs. The double doors leading to the second floor waiting area contained a large panel of transparent glass that allowed us to see inside before we actually opened them. My inadvertent sharp intake of breath coupled with my tightening grip on Mom's arm unconsciously signalled to her that something had caught my eye. There he was, the well attired bogeyman. A cold shudder ran through my spine and hatred and venom almost consumed me. Even though I had been practising the art of calmness, my emotions betrayed my new-found belief. Emotional and psychological abuse is a weird thing; it never really goes away. It just disappears sometimes and simple things act as triggers and then the pain and emotions hit like a ten-ton lorry with all the magnitude that you felt from day one.

The bogey man stood there and looked around and I froze willing him not to see me. His eyes made contact with the Elle shades and he smirked, having found his beating post. As always he looked untouchable and I felt a deep-seated fear. He turned and retreated to a side room with his equally feared person in tow. She did not know, she could not know, that she was described and callously labelled 'wasu gamnage ' by her employer. They were all blinded to the power of the bogeyman. At the time this book is going to publication the court finally recognised his controlling behaviour after telling them he wanted to come to my door daily to collect Son 3. In response he was barred from filing anymore of the numerous aplications he has made over the last two years.

I'll not say much more about the outcome here but I am sure my next book will be filled with many more trips to the courtroom. My story does not end here but I am cognizant of the fact that some day Son 3 will read my story and this part I would love to share with him privately. I have prepared filed and documentary proofs that he can access should he ever ask. I am sure amongst the many issues raised in my story, this may be one point where there will be a lot of discussions about whether he should be told or not. This remains my decision. One salient point worth noting is during my journey, I never denied paternal access or uttered one word to Son 3 about his father as I know a lie is hard to hide and all children eventually grow up and someday he will too.

I however believe in my own self-healing. I am Vinette before anything else, whether daughter, mother, friend or lover. If I am spent then I have nothing to offer anyone in my life. Writing healed me and gave me a reason to push on. I could have buried my story but I chose not to.

Demon eyes

He grinned his nasty grin
Artificial whites glistened unnaturally
Eyes cold and piercing
My unseen tormentor
Covert abuser
Stealth tactics
Legal politics
Infused with misplaced semantics
Radical fanatics
I cower inside
No sign outwardly displayed
I looked into evil
And saw the pain
Like an old wood-burning stove
Crude but effective
Embers fly
Fire stoked
When I looked into his eyes.

Chapter 15
My job!

Not much has been said about my job but I feel it deserves to be mentioned here. I have started on another book *Behind school gates* with a few contributing authors to give an insider look at our schools today.

I am … I was … don't really know right now, but I think I am still a teacher. Teaching, I believe is both a profession and a calling and I suppose it has always been in my blood. My mother is a recently retired teacher and my father for a short while taught. I have sisters, cousins and most of my close friends who are also teachers.

I have always been a teacher and I suspect I will always be a teacher in my heart even if I am not in a formal classroom. Few professions give you the satisfaction of changing someone's life or making someone see the whole world from a completely different perspective as teaching does. I love … loved teaching. As long as I can remember I have been teaching, my career spans over a quarter century and every year has always been my final year in teaching so I could pursue other avenues, but every new school year I would meet another child or class and would decide to see them through their journey. And so one year has rolled into five, then five into ten and before I knew it, I had spent twenty-five years in the teaching profession.

*****

Now, from the outside a school may appear to be just a

place of education where children go to learn and then go home, but if you're seeing a school from the inside then you will realise it has many overlapping layers and, on an even closer inspection, you would realise that each layer is a mere reflection of the other layers.

At the student level, you have the full spectrum of easily recognisable social groups ranging from A* students, the high achievers, to the academically challenged or the students requiring support. We have the popular kids and the wallflowers who never get noticed. There are the usual bullies and the children who are just a few prayers from sainthood, who are simply on earth because they have not yet transitioned. You have the children who will immediately tell the teacher all the wrongs that were committed and those who would prefer to be committed before they tell a teacher anything. There are children who wear the latest brand-name items and those who cannot afford high-end fashion. These are the very basic and broadest categories or social classes that can exist within most schools.

However, unless you work within a school you might be forgiven for missing the very salient and obvious fact that the same groups or strata exist amongst staff and the very same behaviour is exhibited but even more dangerously than amongst the students, because this area I personally believe, does not have the requisite safeguarding checkbox nor does it seem to be as stringently regulated as many may think. The 'top dogs' can make your life so miserable that you need to change school or even your profession. I know many teachers who continue to work in fear or just to pay the bills. They are not very vocal because of possible repercussions and so anything that could be construed as an act of dissent or complaint is kept hidden or discussed in hushed tones in the back of the staffroom or in the parking lots. Just like children when the threat of being discovered surfaces, adults will quickly flee from people who they do not know or anyone who has the ear of the 'top dogs'.

One of my basic guiding philosophies has always been 'you will always find what you're looking for'. If you look for the good in someone then you will always find it, but if you look for the bad, you will find that too. Any conscientious human being would therefore always opt to find the good in people. Unfortunately there are some people who delight in uncovering the bad and feel justified when they can shout about it for the world to see with sadistic indifference to the harm it may inflict on the unlucky person at the end of their quest.

*****

By the time my domestic problem started, I had worked at a certain school in the UK for over five years. I was consistently judged outstanding by Ofsted, senior leaders and all who observed my lessons. I was - am - a phenomenal teacher. I know my craft and deliver it with expertise. However, I was never too popular because I had my own voice and would stand up for myself whenever and wherever I needed to, which was quite frequent. Insecurity of senior practitioners always result in the need for control, compliance and conformity fuelled by fear and threats. In my next book *Behind School Gate*s I will go into more detail about what it was like working in this type of environment. For now I'll just focus on what happened during 2017.

*****

It started some time in April, I started driving into work as I did every morning early but instead of going to my classroom I would sit in my car repeating my daily positive affirmations and listening to some quiet music, just to get in the right frame of mind and face the day. I would literally pull down my rear-view mirror just to check that my smile was intact. Not too wide to seem false but not too small to seem timid either. I had to exude my confidence and strength, no signs of any vulnerability. I practised until I got it right, then I was ready to face any challenge the day would bring. I had to prepare myself for the unexpected or, in my case, the expected.

For the next few days I arrived late but thankfully no one said anything and I did not volunteer any information. By this time I was in temporary accommodation and some mornings I had to collect things from the storage if I had missed closing time the previous day. Occasionally I would turn up to school in the same black trousers for days but thankfully no one noticed or gratefully no one asked about it. At this point I was running on empty but no one knew. I walked like an Amazon and spoke like a queen and everyday before I left home I picked up that big smile and plastered it across my face and I was ready for the world. No cracks I was never the first person in but I was always the first one to leave work under the disapproving gaze of those on duty by the gate. It was a race against time to provide the buffer my children needed. One person in particular would always scowl and completely ignore me as soon as I reached the exit. My 'good afternoon' or nod of acknowledgement was completely ignored, I think he felt that somehow his reaction impacted on me but it honestly did not. In the grand scheme of things he may have thought he was my priority, but if truth be told it did not even make the top twenty on any of my list of priorities in life. I had too many other things going on to even think or worry about other people's opinion of me. I knew who I was and all that I was going through at that moment.

A few days after the last incident at Mr X's house I took the brave decision to talk to someone at work. I knew that emotionally I was feeling the strain and needed some support. For the first time in a while I felt vulnerable and my tears were never very far. Every and anything were triggers for an emotional episode. I would see someone who looked or sounded like Mr X and cry. I would hear certain words and the tears would flow freely. I would smell certain cologne and my heart would start to beat at a rapid pace. I felt as if I was always on the edge.

I went into my HR office and unloaded everything I had been going through. Initially I had planned to just ask for support as I was going through some personal stuff but my emotions were caged up for too long and I started letting go and everything I was experiencing came out. I explained the domestic abuse I had suffered, that I was homeless and struggling at the moment. By the end of my outpouring I begged my employer for help and support. She promised to see what she could do. I asked her to maintain confidentiality with my information although I had strong doubts that my information would be kept confidential. I left the office feeling more stressed than when I entered because I had let my guard down and I feared the next steps. I waited for support but none was forthcoming and I felt like a lamb that had wandered into a cave filled with hungry salivating hyenas, waiting and watching in quiet anticipation for my demise so that they could jump on my body and celebrate.

The constant strain I was under weighed heavily on my shoulders, but now the psychological mind games started as well. Someone would smile or glance at me and I immediately felt that they knew everything about my life. Miraculously I still managed to maintain my smile.

Against my instincts I went back a few weeks later and asked for some flexibility at work with my classes and workload but once again nothing was done. Well that's not exactly true. On the last day of summer term , of the ten teachers who were allocated Year 7 tutor groups, I was the only one to be taken off the Year 7 pastoral team and given a Year 10 group who were very unsettled and had a history of misbehaviour. This group would certainly test me. The change would undoubtedly add more stress to my already stressful situation and I could not help wondering if this was a deliberate and calculated move. I was determined that they would not get that satisfaction downfall and that became a bit of motivation to press on.

I made it to the end of the term and swiftly left on the last day of term, handing in a change-of-address form. I could almost envisage the hushed conferences that occurred over that form. In one academic year I had 'lived' in six different places including hotels. The summer holiday beckoned and I nervously stepped to meet it.

*****

September 2017 and I was still in an heightened emotional state and feeling very fragile. I missed the first day of school and turned up on day two to face any challenges that would come my way. I was relieved that the first day of term passed without any disaster and I was grateful. Sometimes when you're in the darkness of life, each little moment that brought some light is magnified and celebrated. The first few weeks flew by without incident but by then my personal life was still unsettled as Mr X had now filed for full custody and was kind enough to allow me extensive visits. This meant court and my anxiety levels increased.

Now anyone who knows me, knows my children are my life. I could lose the world but I would give my life for any one of my children. I love them fiercely and when I perceive any form of threat, my rationale becomes affected.

I walked into work and this time I went straight to the HR's office. She was in. After she asked me to come in, she offered me a seat and I sat down. To hide my nervousness, I sat on both hands. 'Yes?' she asked, looking at me with a bit of concern. Where would I start? I closed my eyes, took a deep breath and I could hear the voice and the words coming out but it was robotic and monotonous. I spoke so quickly I forgot to breath and was only reminded I had to breath when my voice started going squeaky and then stopped. All at once it seemed as if my tears were being dammed by my voice box and as soon as I stopped speaking and starting gasping for breath the deluge of tears descended. The HR manager reached for a box of tissues and I gratefully accepted a few sheets.

When sufficient time had passed and the level of awkwardness had been reduced to an acceptable level I started speaking again. I explained that I needed some support and I reminded her that I wanted my circumstance to remain confidential and on a strictly need to know basis and she agreed to keep it private. However she once again explained that due to budgetary constraints the service that could provide some support were expensive and they are external and well she was doubtful that. . . . . she allowed her sentence to tail off punctuated by a shrug of the shoulder. She then went on to explain that Occupational Health might be able to offer some service but it would take too long. I went back mid September to reiterate my need for support and was told the school was in a budgetary deficit and would not be in a position to afford that kind of support. HR instead wrote in a piece of paper, with some free services I could access to help my children if I needed it. Disappointed I left the office but smiling because it was all I could do.

I continued to follow my usual morning routines in my car each morning before I headed to my teaching room. I had gotten into the habit of quietly locking myself in my room with the lights switched off. This was multi-purpose and it served me well. Firstly it allowed me some quiet time where I could switch off, which were needed more and more those days as I could not sleep at nights anymore. I was always thinking what might happen next or thinking about how I could possible escape from my mental anguish. I knew Mr X was not yet finished with me. No one noticed and if they did, no one said anything. Inside my head was so busy and it took a lot of energy which meant most times I was absolutely exhausted. During those times I would post inspirational messages on various social-media platforms and people commented and responded. The truth was, those messages were just for me to remind myself that I had to keep going because if I stopped I was certain to go under. It was like that story of the mouse who fell into some cream and kept pedalling until he churned that cream into butter. If he had stopped at any point he would have certainly drowned and I was also busy making butter.

The second reason I locked myself in was just to avoid everyone. For months I had walked around just a word or an action away from breaking into tears. There were a few difficult moments when a child or an adult in passing would say something and it would cut me to the core but I said nothing. I would find some inspirational music and play it over and over and over again until I could self motivate myself. This was my comfort until a staff member in the adjoining room reported me to the headteacher that I was playing music that had nothing to do with my lesson.

One evening during a meeting, my line manager proudly proclaimed to the room, 'ah Vinette, only her body is here, her mind is gone!' and everyone including myself smiled. How could she know how accurate her statement was? I was a mere shell walking around. It might have been funny to everyone but to me my mind was on my son that had Asperger's and was away from home for the first time at university, my next son who was feeling depressed, a child custody battle, financial distress caused by my uninvited court battles, domestic abuse and the list goes on. It was an absolute miracle that even my body was there; my mind was a bonus.

I said nothing, but that ever-present smile that acted like a dam for my emotions quickly and robotically plastered itself on my face, just a simple smile to keep what was left of me inside and to keep the world outside. It was my safety net.

Another random incident involved my mobile phone in a room full of my colleagues. Throughout the day I constantly received messages from solicitors and from my mom who kept a close eye on my children. I was always on edge so my mobile phone never left my body outside of lesson times. What if someone needed me and I could not be reached? Would I be seen as a bad mother and lose my children? I could not risk anything going wrong. Sometimes even when you are the victim you start to second guess everything you do or say. My phone was also my writing pad where all my thoughts, dreams, notes and desires were recorded and I had to write to maintain my sanity and have an outlet. I had to write. It was free therapy. So I sat in a meeting writing each point as my brain was full at this point and there was literally no space for any additional information so if it was not written it would be forgotten. I started jotting down bullet points and the staff member leading the meeting saw me. 'Put away your phone ' he ordered aggressively.

I responded, 'I'm only taking notes.'

'You are so impolite!' He loudly labelled me in front of everyone. I could not respond because once again I could feel the emotions fighting to escape and I just had to keep them in check. I simply smiled to reinforce the dam.

Isn't it intriguing how people treat others without ever stopping to think they might need a kind word or a hug. If someone looks nice, acts confident and is always smiling, everyone assumes everything must be ok. Sometimes these people are the ones that need love the most. Arrogance, anger and self assuredness, I have come to realise, are sometimes the biggest signals that say 'I need help.'

I also started placing things in boxes and would not think about more than a few things at a time. It was one of my many coping strategies that I employed or self-administered to get me through it all. I regularly spoke to my GP and he periodically referred me to some agencies that could help but I could never find the courage to call or book an appointment. I just didn't want to share any more. I felt embarrassed and I wanted the illusion that I had everything under control to remain intact. I had gone to my employers for help and received none. I did not trust anyone and I did not want to repeat my story.

I remember the first day I realised I was not coping. A student from my tutor group asked a question and I answered in a tone that was not aggressive but not too friendly either. I would teach but I nervously listened for footsteps on the corridors and I always imagined that those footsteps were taking some bad news to me and my heart raced. I would frequently ask my technicians or another staff member to watch my class for about two minutes, lying that I had to use the toilets when in actual fact I was having mini panic attacks, or a child would say something benign and I would feel the tears welling up. I knew I had to ask for help but I was still hesitant. I figured I had the charade under control.

*****

As I was leaving work one afternoon my eyes met a key player at work. I smiled but it was a smile from the lips. My eyes did not smile. I knew, and he knew that I knew, it was just an unspoken understanding that I was not his cup of tea and he certainly was not mine. He looked at me as if he was waiting, knowing somehow that something was about to happen to me. I walked down the long corridors to the HR office and stood outside the door. I paused for a few seconds then gathered the courage to knock. No answer. I knocked again leaning forward to peek inside to see if she was sitting there but the office was empty. A sense of elation and relief filled me and I quickly walked away telling myself I had made the first step.

Each night I would write, a few words sometimes, or

thousands depending on my mood. Each night I wrote about the future where I could dictate whatever I wanted to happen. I wrote about speaking in front of ten thousand on the O2 arena stage, I then flew around the world giving motivational talks to rapturous applause and standing ovations. I smiled at my new life and was grateful for the pain because I could now appreciate what I now had.. It was my fantasy but fantasies can become realities. I believe.

*****

For several years my behavioural management was exemplary but my lack of focus, lack of sleep and the myriad of problems made me weak and I struggled. To further add a bit of stress, students with behavioural problems were transferred to my class. I complained to my line manager and several senior managers but nothing. I felt as if the world and everything had dropped onto my shoulders but still I managed to wear that smile.

I will not go into much details here … yet! Maybe Book 2 when all is resolved.

I remember thinking, in this age where stress and mental health are topical subjects, it is remarkable that no one actually cares before; they respond after.

My job!

Do you care?

Yes, you receive me in your employ
But when I need help you choose to act coy
You judge me by my confident walk and ever-present smile
And conclude that I don't fit your acceptable profile
I tell you I am struggling and need some support
Instead you watch from the side and collate your reports
You heap more pressure on my head
And give little help, turning your back instead.
You give me more than I could carry
Without remorse or even a sorry
Yes, you tried to tear me down
All because I wear a smile instead of a frown !

*****

Someone else asked again that day, 'Vinette have you left teaching?'

'Yes!' I lied with a well rehearsed smile. It was easier to keep the illusion, not just for the questioner but for myself. Over this tumultuous period I had started reading books that would bring some calm to my kind. I read the Bible, the akashic records, Anam Cara, various motivational and inspirational books that provided a buzz although temporary from my current situation.

I was suspended from my job on December 6, 2017 amidst several allegations including:

Making inappropriate comments to students.

No doctors note for one day's absence (legally we require a doctor's certificate after seven days self-certification).

Facebook posts at times when I was allegedly in class.

Playing music in class.

As I was in the middle of fighting for my son, settling my eldest with special needs, settling into a new home and providing statements to the police I thought there was no way I could take another battle at that time. My energy was completely divested and near depletion.

Instead I offered my resignation in early January. My offer was met with an email outlining all that would be said about me if anyone ever asked for a reference in the future and insisted it had to be an immediate resignation.

I took the night to just sleep. I just blanked everything from my mind and slept. I woke up the next day and decided to focus on one battle at a time. After years of teaching in the UK I was not prepared to lose my reputation and career because I knew all the allegations were contrived and false. Even though my union recommended I resign instead of risking a dismissal on my record, I insisted I wanted to fight the allegations and that was conveyed to the school.

The headteacher then unexpectedly submitted his resignation mid way through the process. I am not making any links between my situation and his resignation but please read my next book which is written in both white and black ink.

Occupational Health deemed me unfit to work and so my investigatory hearing was held in my absence. I decided to attend the formal disciplinary meeting however.

Immediately before the meeting my union representative took me aside to explain that the school wanted to offer me a great reference and a two-week period to resign. I was dumbstruck. He then went on to explain that news that I was writing a book had surfaced and there was growing concern regarding the content. I reassured my union representative that I would not tell any lies but my story is my story and I would not entertain any request to be silenced.

On hindsight, because the conversation was verbal and basically my word against someone else's, I cheekily emailed my union rep to ask a random question and he confirmed in writing that the school wanted me to be 'circumspect' in what I decided to write.

What had caused this sudden change, this sudden turn around? Well a week before the meeting I had regained my faith and fasted and prayed daily for deliverance with the help of Shepherd Dele. He assured me, that just as for Daniel, the mouths of the lions would remain shut.

That episode provided a steep learning curve. There were many other things that were said but I will leave the details for a next time.

However, it made me realise once again that people can literally plan your downfall with little regard for you as a person. One can look at this incident in many ways. If I was such a terrible teacher who warranted a dismissal from the profession, then why would a headteacher disregard all the evidence and provide a good reference for me to work in another educational institution? Other than the fact that

I chose to write a book, what changed and brought about such a harsh U-turn? Does this mean you are at the mercy of headteachers and whether or not they like or dislike you? Are there no regulations that prevent schools from acting in this way?

I am grateful for the way things eventually worked out but I learnt lessons that will be with me throughout my life.

Chapter 16
A mother's perspective

Have you ever had this persistent feeling that something isn't right? That somewhere in the shadows are lurking some sinister secrets. Well, if you are anything like me you would try to identify the problem, find the solution so everything becomes perfect. Yes, I have been called a perfectionist and a diplomat by my friends. Diplomat, well – yes, but 'perfectionist' is not an adjective I would ascribe to myself. If, from reading this chapter, you identify any perfectionist traits then maybe I am. It is very difficult for me to deliberately hurt anyone and even when people hurt me I generally use some stories or proverbs to make them understand what they have done. I don't hate anyone, only the wrong things they do. Notwithstanding, sometimes the message just past over some people's heads. However I realise that your friends can identify your traits much better than you can. Among my other attributes is the deep love I have for my family. As a matter of fact this love supersedes everything except my love of God. There is nothing that I won't do for my children. I just want them to be happy, achieve their goals and be independent.

So when my eldest daughter asked me to return to the UK to give her my support, I had no second thoughts. My four children and I are as close as peas in a pod. My daughter wanted to hone her skills in public speaking, therefore she would be travelling around the country competing in different toastmasters clubs. I knew this would not be easy as she is also a full-time science teacher.

A week later, I arrived in England and travelled from Gatwick to Bedford. I walked into a sprawling five-bedroom house with most of the comforts that anyone needs. It was richly furnished with all the modern appliances and furniture. The decor was superb. There was a huge summer house outside and manicured lawns. Her youngest son's father had bought the property and somehow persuaded her to move in with him and share living accommodation. I was not in agreement but sometimes you have to allow children to make their own decisions.

An unsettled feeling lingered in my stomach but I just could not explain it. Little did I know of the sinister events that were about to unfold and transform our lives into a nightmare. I have always known my l Mr X to be a showman. He does the big things that people will see because he thrives on praise. For example, he will pay for his children to go to a private school but he finds it most difficult to give them regular support. He aspired to be among the elite and he pretends to be one of them. In order to convince himself and others he will boast about how many disciplines he studied at university. According to him, he has studied law, medicine, journalism, sociology...

He would often indulge in conversation with such confidence that an ordinary person listening would be in awe. However if you listen keenly, you will soon realise that there is no real substance in his coversation. For example the word expletive becomes 'expeletive'. He was so brave that he would challenge two experienced teachers on any subject. On a few occasions I stood up to him and held my ground for what I knew was correct. My daughter would look at me anxiously and whisper, 'Mom, just agree with him because you can't change his views.' I knew my daughter deserved better but she was grown. I did not like the arrangement. I would have preferred her to be living happily in a cabin than there; it was just not a comfortable setting. But I said nothing. I just supported her where I was needed.

About a week after I had settled into the routine of daily life, I began to have this terrible feeling that something just wasn't right. The first thing I noticed was there were two large dining tables. One was in the kitchen area where the children would eat most of the time, the other was in the conservatory for the adults. There were two lounges, one of which was locked off and the children dared not enter that area unless their mother was with them. This I found strange.. In all my years of bringing up children I have never separated them from the main family areas. How are they going to learn dining etiquette if they do not eat with adults and so see how things are done? Secondly, two of my grandsons spent most days in their rooms when my son-in-law was at home. The third grandson who also happen to be his son could go anywhere he pleased. My son-in-law called him the 'Boss'. If the other boys happen to be downstairs, as soon as he walked through the door everyone retreated to their rooms.

Having noticed this behaviour on several occasions, I mentioned my concerns to my daughter. Her response was,

'Mom, please take care of them when I am not around. Let me work some things out.' These words put me on high alert and I had my antennae positioned. In other words I got into mother-hen mode. Another peculiar thing I noticed was the sticking of yellow post-it notes all over the house. They were on furniture, doors, windows and the desks in his office. One day my curiosity got the better of me and I asked him why they were there. He informed me that they were markers and reminders about house rules. and the shoddy work done by his workmen.

Now I know full well I am not a painter or a carpenter but when he tried to point out what was wrong with the men's work I just couldn't see any major issues. Admittedly there was a minuscule scratch on one of the cabinets. A scratch so small that you needed a microscope to see it clearly. When I told him that I could barely see the scratch his reply was, 'I can be very brutal'. One senior workman was summoned byMr X, to go and inspect some of his office furniture which had been fitted by his subordinates. When the gentleman came, he was not at home so the workman had to sit and wait for almost ninety minutes. The gentleman said he had to drive ninety miles and must return that day. When Mr X showed me the reason he had the man come to the house I was appalled. I said, 'Is that all?'

His response was, 'it is enough and if it isn't done to my satisfaction I will continue to call until they spend every penny I have paid them.' Such was his callousness that he watched as the men did the work and never said that was not how he wanted it done. He claimed it was not his responsibility to correct them.

Mr X placed a massive box at one of the entrances to the kitchen which forced everyone to walk the long distance through the children's sitting room and the conservatory in order to gain entry. When asked for the reason he said another workman had not done his job properly. I spent almost three months there and that workman has never returned.

He also instituted several rules for the family members to adhere to. Certain foods could not be eaten in his house and in order to ensure that they consume only those foods that he approved of, he would often search the bins and the rooms for any evidence of disobedience. One morning after his search, he told me that he had found sweet wrappers in my middle grandson's room and in the bin. I smiled.

He wanted to know my opinion so I told him moderation was key. He grunted and moved on. As a result of these draconian rules I noticed several behaviours in the children. If they needed a snack they would take it when he wasn't looking and hide it in their pockets. This was wrong on so many levels. I asked my middle grandson why he was hiding food and he told me that Mr X would give him the evil eye if he saw him eating snacks. This hurt me to the core so I told him to tell me when he needed something and I would get it for him. My grandson gave me a smile of relief.

Every morning, religiously, at about four o clock I could hear Dranoel's muffled voice. At first, I thought it was just light talk since my daughter usually gets up early to prepare for work. One morning the voice seemed to get a little louder so I asked my daughter if there was a problem. I am a very sensitive person and I didn't want to be an inconvenience to him. She assured me that it was nothing to do with me; he was complaining about the boys again. I asked her what they could have done for him to complain every morning. She said there was always something. Later it got worse, the voices got louder so I went out of my room to see what was the matter. I saw Mr X standing at his door while my daughter stood in the passage. Apparently he had told her last night that he did not want my nineteen-year-old grandson living in the home anymore. This was just vile because my grandson was studying for his A levels. It was a deliberate effort to destabilise the young man. Vinette was very private and I sensed there was more but she would not say anymore.

Mr X's diet was meat, vegetables and fruits because he was diabetic and those were the foods he wanted us to partake of. One day he brought home some massive slices of fish. They were the most unappetising protein I have ever seen. He told me I could prepare some of it. I prepared it and gave it to him and informed him that I was not well so I wouldn't have any. He feasted on that fish every day. When he noticed that no one was partaking of it he declared one day that it was the kind of fish that was eaten by royalty . I told him I would remain a peasant.

One day Mr X brought home a bike for his son who was very elated and began to ride round and round outside.

He was having such fun but his brother who was twelve years old and with whom he had a close relationship had to watch him having fun from the conservatory. Vinette came home and realised that grandson number two was left out of the fun so she went and bought a bike for him the next day. As soon as she left for work the next day, Mr X began to complain that she was deeply in debt and he did not know where she got the money from to buy a bike. I can only imagine that this was a deliberate attempt on his part to separate the brothers because a few weeks later he began to complain that the boys were leaving tyre tracks on his summer house so they were not allowed to ride outside any more. He then took his son riding in the park while his brother had to stay at home.

One afternoon my daughter came home and sat in the children's living room. The other family members were upstairs hiding.. After about fifteen minutes, I noticed that she hadn't come looking for us as she always did, so I went downstairs. She wasn't there but Mr X was in the garden tending his plants. My daughter had left in her car. I called her on her mobile and she told me she would be back soon. About an hour elapsed before she returned. She came straight to my room to apologise for not coming to see me. I could clearly see that something wasn't right with her. Now she is a very private person so there are some things that she will not willingly divulge to me but I pushed her to tell me what was wrong. Apparently she had come home with a bottle of coke in her bag and Mr X went into her bag to retrieve it then told her she was violating his rule. I saw flashes of red. I drank about a gallon of water before I was nearing a calm state. She begged me not to confront him and I didn't.

Although I have retired I still like to stay active, so in the mornings when my daughter left for work, I would do some house work. One morning he looked at me and announced, 'I wish your daughter were like you!'

I asked, 'What do you mean?'

'Well, you are so neat and orderly. Every morning you tidy the house and you keep everything in its correct place', he replied.

'Are you saying my daughter doesn't tidy the house?' I asked.

'Well she is your child,' he replied.

I reminded him that my daughter had a job outside of the home so it was difficult to keep up with the work at home and that was the reason I was helping. This was the beginning of a barrage of negative criticism of my child. I never knew that a man could be so callous to someone. In Jamaica parlance you would call such men 'Maama Man'.

Every morning as soon as she left the house he had something to say about her or some complaints about two of the boys. He told me that Grandson Number 2 had turned up the heating above the limit he had set it for and caused it to malfunction. I asked him if he was sure of this and he told me the child had admitted it. He said this was going to cost him a whole lot of money. I told him how sorry I was but I was happy he admitted it. Later that day the electrician came to look at the system and while I stood there I heard the him telling Mr X that it was some faulty wiring that caused the malfunction. When the electrician left I said to him, ' so it was faulty wiring then?' His response was, 'he has no idea what he is talking about. We will allow him to think it is faulty wiring but I know that it is because Grandson Number 2 overrode the system.'

That weekend I understood why my daughter was reluctant to do the housework when he was present. She was cleaning the stove so she took the trays outside to wash them. He followed her outside demonstrating how they should be cleaned and put to dry. As if that wasn't enough he followed her back inside while she was cleaning a glass-top table. He began to explain how to use the hoover to clean it. I had to exit the room as quickly as I could, lest I open my mouth and tell him a few choice words.

After a while I got so angry I told my daughter everything one day. Surprisingly she said she was planning to leave but she didn't want to do so immediately because her eldest son was doing his A levels and she had been saving. She asked me to ignore it a little longer. She said I was to pretend and agree with everything he said. There and then I made the decision not to respond to him when he complained but I would not agree with him! My stance led to him threatening me in a subtle manner.

One day after my daughter left for work, he invited me to go with him to Kettering to see a doctor who does acupuncture. On the way he began to criticise my eldest grandson so badly that I struggled to honour my pledge not to say anything. It was so bad that the tears started to well up in my eyes. Soon they overflowed and began to form small rivulets down my cheeks. He looked at me and smiled. That was it. If he said one more bad thing about my grandchild I would let him have the full force of my tongue.

His next words took me by surprise because I could not make any connection to his verbal assault on my grandson. 'I would never enter a competition,' he stated. 'I prefer to work for an honest living.'

Without knowing where he was coming from and spurred by my intense dislike for the man I offered an opposing argument. 'This is a competitive world,' I replied, 'so that's a silly comment.' I went on to enlighten him about competitions I knew he had entered when he bid for his job.

It then dawned on me the reason he had made that statement. My daughter had won fourteen trophies in Toastmasters and was going to represent the UK and Ireland in Vancouver. Jealousy was eating away at his core so this despicable being went on the attack. We travelled for several miles before he said another word and when he did it brought forcibly home to me how vindictive one person can be. 'You see these hands,' he announced, 'They are lethal. I can break a brick with them and I can be quite brutal.'

I gave him the infamous Jamaican look because I know he would have to take me by surprise. I thank God every day that his threats were did not materialise or I would be writing this chapter from one of Her Majesty's hotels.

*****

For some unknown reasonMr X continued to take out his anger and jealousy on my nineteen-year-old grandson. He had used a special material for the kitchen floor. If the floor got wet it was likely to be permanently damaged. I had to ask myself which rational thinking individual would use such material for a home where children live? Anyway my grandson was cooking one day and the oil spilled. After much ranting and raving, Mr X meted out his punishment, which was a ban from the kitchen.

This was a predicament. If my grandson should not enter the kitchen and should not eat in his room where was he to eat? I pointed this out but Mr X gave no response, After a few weeks of my grandson eating in my daughter's car, he reluctantly allowed him to eat in the kitchen but he couldn't touch the stove. The young man had to go downstairs at five o clock every morning before he awoke to get his breakfast then rush back to his room. 'Dear God,' I prayed, 'take this feeling of hate from me. I have lived a very sheltered life and have never met anyone so calculating, vindictive and cruel.' Every fibre in my being despised his evil ways.

Before I continue, let me use this opportunity to commend my eldest grandson for being a very fine, extremely cultured and disciplined nineteen-year-old. During all of this difficult situation, he remained calm most of the time. He had the utmost respect for me and his mother and I love him worlds without end. As parents his mother and I encouraged him to try to remain calm and not to respond to any provocations because he was now ~Mr X's main target. Mr X picked on him relentlessly and as a result I decided to follow my grandchild around the house.

On one particular morning Mr X was also up early. Whether he did this deliberately or not, I do not know but the tranquillity of the morning was suddenly interrupted by his loud shouting. 'Mom! Debrah, (Debrah is my youngest daughter) please come down here!'

Without a second thought we grabbed our robes and rushed downstairs like bullets from a gun. When we got to the kitchen, we saw my grandson sitting calmly at the dining table having scrambled eggs and toast. We inquired of Mr X what the matter was. He yelled, 'We told this boy not to use the stove and he has disobeyed the rule.' Without speaking I calmly walked over to the stove and felt the burners. They were ice cold.

I turned to my grandson and asked him how he had cooked his eggs and he answered, 'The micro-wave.'

Instead of apologising, Mr X looked straight at me and uttered angrily, 'do you hear how he speaks to an adult?' My youngest daughter and I just turned and, without saying a word, went back to bed.

Mr X continued his reign of terror for another two months.

One afternoon my grandson returned from college and said he stood outside for about fifteen minutes. We did not know he had returned. I was going down the stairs when I heard Mr X said, 'why don't you come inside?'

My grandson replied, 'but you are standing in the way.'

Apparently Mr X saw him coming and stood with his

hand across the door to block him from entering the house. When he heard me coming down the stairs, that was the time he invited him into the house. It is these devious behaviours that cause me to struggle to separate the hatred of the deeds from the individual. Since I grew up in a Christian home and I also brought up my children to fear God and live according to his dictates, I decided to have another conversation with my daughter. I told her we had to leave this man's place because I was getting to be a very angry person. Certainly we could find somewhere for my grandsons to be comfortable. Surely it would be better to be in another environment with less grandeur and be happy. At this point I noticed that my daughter looked very worried. 'What's the matter?' I enquired. 'All we need is the rent and the security deposit. Surely, we can afford that.' My daughter looked at me with troubled eyes then informed me that the crafty fox, who was had carted off all her furniture and her belongings to his sister's house. Everything she had worked hard to purchase over fifteen years was gone.

Words cannot express my shock at this point. I was speechless for a while.

'Call her, text her, email her!' I shouted after I recovered. 'We have to get them back.' I watched her write an email to that woman - who never replied. We were stuck.

The unloved

Bitter, twisted and broken inside
Dead eyes reflect the tears cried
Hollow and dead from within
Masked by a semi toothless grin
Dead mind, dead heart, dead soul
Emotions stone cold
They walk around seeking those that smile
To break the spirit and crush the inner child
No one can love these demons
You lose your soul if you think you can

A few weeks later I was hanging out some clothes for my daughter when Mr X slowly walked by. 'You have now become the helper, ' he blurted out. I smiled because that was all the ammunition I had left.

Oh, how he hated to hear our laughter. Laughter was our antidote, our comfort, our therapy. I told my grandsons funny stories and we laughed; we sang funny songs and laughed some more. It kept us sane but made him mad with anger. He told me that afternoon that some men were coming to work in his office so he was asking me to clear it for him. I didn't do it. I was a helper for my children not for him. When he returned and saw it wasn't done he looked at me and declared, 'you are a very feisty one, aren't you.'

I replied, 'quite right.' He cleared the room all by himself but things got even more tense after that.

Most Sundays Mr X went off to play golf so everyone looked forward to a relaxing day. We were sitting in the children's living room when my eldest daughter disappeared. She spied him coming and raced upstairs. We were trapped. He walked through the door, said good evening to us and went out into the garden. That was our cue to flee the downstairs area so we raced upstairs. Approximately fifteen to twenty minutes later we heard him speaking loudly downstairs. My youngest daughter asked that we go down as it seemed as if they were having an argument. We crept downstairs into the children's living room. There I saw my daughter sitting on the sofa with her dress ripped at the shoulder and Mr X standing at the entrance to the conservatory. My daughter was crying. 'What's the matter?' I inquired. Mr X did not respond but my daughter looked at us and said she was going to the police station.

'They will only arrest you!' he shouted.

She hurriedly left in her car and he followed in his car.

The rest of the evening of May 27 unfolded in slow motion but within a day we had moved out of the house and into a hotel.

*****

Two days later she finally told me what had happened that afternoon and all she had endured. I cried.

As a mother there are certain things you wish would never happen to your children and if they happen you feel lost and vulnerable. He was arrested that night and the following day we moved out of his house. The main author may tell you in more detail all she endured in that hell-hole and the struggle we went through afterwards to find somewhere suitable to live. It is her story to tell. This is only from my perspective. Suffice it to say there were myriad other incidents I could have recorded but I think this is.

Although our life at Mr X's home was a nightmare, surprisingly there were a few happy times but I have deliberately left them until last because I want to end on a happy note. My daughter encouraged me to write in order to cleanse my soul because I had become very bitter towards that man. After all, whatever happened to him in his formative years must have had this negative impact on him because he was not only horrible to us, he was also very obnoxious to his older daughter because she had disobeyed him and married outside of her race. He told me that if they had a child that child would never be his grandchild. How could that child not be his grandchild? Now I only feel pity for him and hope that one day he will repent of his ways. I can only hope he reads this book and realise how deeply his actions can hurt other people.

We went on holiday to Cornwall, a place I had never been before. As I said this was one of the good times we all had so I will not stain it with anything negative that happened there. I will only say lovely things. We stayed in a lodge. It was superb. We took fantastic photographs and dined at unique restaurants. For this I am very grateful and I wish him the repentance he deserves.

I am extremely grateful to God that with all the conflict, my grandson passed his A levels and is now studying at university. My other two grandsons are with us although Mr X filed for custody of the youngest. We are keeping calm and facing each day with great expectations.

Chapter 17
A sister's perspective

Vinette my sister is a very loving and caring person. Miserable and moody? One hundred and one percent. But she was always very kind. If you ask her for a pound and that was the last pound she had, Vinette would give it to you with no argument.

She would go out of her way to help someone. She offered her elderly neighbours lifts to the doctors when their car refused to start, even though she did not know them. That is the kind of person she is. Another occasion that my sister showed good will and all that jazz was when her ex-partner Mr. X needed to have surgery on his eyes she was kind enough to take him to the hospital and then back home. Even though he lied to her about several things and these range from claims he bought a house near the private school he wanted my nephew to attend. He got my nephew who was the youngest at the time into the private school and made promises to move close to the school. But this was all lies. That is how forgiving my sister is.

I never knew how evil and conniving he could be until 2016 when everything was set in motion. Let's start before we moved into the house which was known as the hell h***.

Living in a close-knit family we wished the best and the success for everyone and we cheered them on from the side-lines.

It was the summer of 2016 and I had just moved in with my big sister who sometimes could pass for my mother because I value her opinion above all else. If there was a decision to be made about anything we would sit down and discuss it in detail on what we should do and how it would benefit us as a family. On this one specific meeting, my sister was discussing moving houses as we had gotten notice from the landlord and considered living with the father of her youngest child. After great deliberation, we drew up some terms and conditions. These may have been discussed with you by the main author.

After careful deliberations, we decided that, yes, we would move in with my nephew's father on a temporary basis. The moving date was set for the autumn half-term 2016. This worked perfectly for me and my sister because we both had half-term and we would be able to pack and get everything ready for the big move. But first, he insisted on taking us on a half-term holiday which was welcomed by everyone. My nephews, especially the oldest one was reluctant but came eventually.

I joined my sister on the holiday on the third day. Even though I only had three days there, I was grateful for them to invite me along for the get-away. On arrival, I found it exciting and very interesting because it was a new experience and a new place. It was wonderful being on the holiday and everyone was getting along. He seemed to have changed and I relaxed a bit more.

However, on a few occasions if he anyone picked selected an item of high value when we went shopping, he always talked about how much it cost and how he had to work for it. I always put this down to differences in culture or the way he was brought up but it began to put a downer on the time away and it always made me second guess everything I did around him I would sneak away from the group and do my own thing. I didn't want to upset the balance of things and say something to my sister. This was the first of many times that I felt discomfort and annoyance in his presence.

It was a week since we had the holiday and they were running behind in getting the other house done so we could move in officially. I did not know what it was at the time but my back was up and I wanted to tell my sister that I had changed my mind about the move. However, I knew that she had worked hard in life and I thought that she deserved some help sothere would be less financial pressure on her for a while. The main reason I kept changing my mind was his constant jabs about the things that my sister kept, from an old baby blanket to Christmas tree. In my eyes, if you care for someone you should value what they like and want to keep. These comments were made more than once during the move to the new home but always when my sister was absent.

The moving day came and went. It was not even a month before his attitude towards the children started to change. One morning I was helping to pack things out in the kitchen when he came in and looked around to see if my sister was in earshot. When he noticed that she was not in the room and it was only me and my youngest nephew he said, 'there are going to be some rules for this kitchen, starting today: no children allowed in this room and if you need something you will have to ask an adult.' I found this outrageous in restricting a child from opening the cupboard and getting something they need. I also knew that he would not do it himself but deflected the request to me or my sister. I found him to be a dictator and an annoying person. I didn't see why he could not discuss these things beforehand because the children could not process the rules overnight that he dictated. I think he believed that children should be seen and not heard. Here is the list of rules he made:

- Children should not be in the kitchen without an adult present.
- Children should be in their living room and not disturb the adults in the other room.

Well this backfired because on many occasions he was the only adult sitting in the adult room as everyone else found it more comfortable sitting with the children in their living room. We all gravitated to this room because it was warm and full of love. He did not like the idea that we all were in the kids room so he would hover over the door ways trying to look intimidating and would make remarks that the room was for the children alone and not adults. We still ignored him and congregated in that room although my sister would sometimes go and sit with him. It always felt as if she was taking a bullet for the team.

- Children should eat at a different table from the adults.
- Children could not enter either parents' bedrooms even in case of emergencies.

I found this rule ridiculous because the boys are very close to their mother and would go to her for help. I thought what if the children were ill and unable to call their mother? They still managed to sneak into her room sometimes when Mr X was locked in his room and they heard snores.

- People are only allowed to open the cupboard five times during the day.

- The rules of the house did not only apply to the inside but made their way to the outside. He demanded that we park in a certain way and made up a lie that the person who takes care of the neighbourhood had told him about the parking arrangement. . However, I soon realized that this was a lie when other neighbours parked in the same wrong position many evenings.

- Another rule was that Boy 1, who is the eldest, was not allowed to make his breakfast or even prepare a dish for himself. At the time I thought that he didn't like Boy 1 very much. Even if Boy 1 was close to the kitchen he would get accused of using the hob. There was this one particular Saturday morning where my sister left early for a competition when I heard Mr. X calling my mother's name and mine down stairs at around 6:30 am in the morning. This was a day I normally lay in and got some rest from the usual early morning start. At that moment in time, I was thinking, God, what does this man want? My mother and I shared a look and made our way downstairs. When we arrived in the kitchen I saw my nephew eating his breakfast calmly. Mr. X said to us that Boy 1 was 'being disrespectful and was not following the rules. He clearly used the stove. When I asked him how he made his breakfast he said he cooked it.' He turned to us and pointed that Boy 1 was disobeying the rules. My mother and I looked around the kitchen and the hob was not even hot; there was no oil splatter on the stove itself. Mr. X demanded that we asked Boy1 how he made the meal. It was obvious that he used the microwave but my mother asked anyways and the answer she got was that he used the microwave. With this answer, I turned to exit the kitchen without making a comment but he stood there in front of the only escape from the kitchen. He stood there still insisting that Boy 1 used the stove. My mother marched over to the stove and touched the rings and they were cold and proved that he did not use the stove. While she did this I moved towards thc door and said 'excuse me' but he refused to move so I had to push past him. I did not care that it was rude I just wanted to go back to bed. I was not worried about what my mother found by the stove because my nephew never told a lie about how he does things.

- Another one of his rules was that food and shoes should not be taken upstairs. This was not a bad rule. However the problem was that he would search everyone's rooms when they were not in the house. I had a suspicion that he went into the room I was staying in and removed small items. This can't be proven for definite but I have seen him going into the children's room and searching Boy 2's bed.

There were many more rules that I can't remember right now. But I found that he wanted to know what everyone was doing and would use every tactic in the book to find out. An example of this was when I had a doctor's appointment after work. I decided that I was going to pop back to the house and ask my sister to tell me where the doctor's surgery was. I rushed into the house and put my work things away as instructed and then went into the kitchen. Mr. X was sitting in the kitchen with my sister. I said the normal greetings with a fake smile. I then went to the sink and washed up my lunch kit. By this time he had left the room; I turned to my sister and asked her where the surgery was because I had not had the chance to explore the area. We were talking for a while when I noticed that it was time to leave and go to the surgery. As I was about to rush out of the kitchen door there was Mr. X blocking my exit. He asked where I was going and I informed him that I was going out. This did not quench the thirst for knowledge about where I was going so he decided to put his hand across the doorway so I could not pass. I refused to tell him where I was going until my sister said that I was going to be late for the appointment and asked him to move his hand so that I could pass. In some situations, I am very diplomatic while in others I am a bull in a china shop and this incident was one of the times I would have lost my manners and told him to move rudely if my sister had not intervened.

He did not like it when my mother, my sister and I got together to discuss projects or reminisce about the past. He always seemed to have done the same thing but one step better than us. I found this to be very petty.

One of his favourite pastimes during my time in the house was to falsely accuse my sister of not paying for Boy 2's school fees. Once he saw me sitting with Boy 3 in the kids' lounge and called me to complain like a fish monger. He said to me, 'Vinette has not paid any money in the joint account for Boy 2; she only put money in there once and it was only £500. But I knew this to be a lie, because she does her best and goes above and beyond to provide for her children. I don't know why he would want to slander her name to me. The only reason I think is because I did not talk back. I wasn't openly rude to him because he owned the house and could kick me out at any time.

When he started to pressurize my eldest nephew about his eating habits and what he would or would not allow in the house, he bought a book that states what people with Asperger's/autism should eat. I found it frustrating that he was picking on my nephew. I told him that people with autism are different and one size does not fit all but he did not understand this.

On many occasion he would spy and see what we were eating. Due to this, my nephews felt extremely uncomfortable, I could remember one occasion where he was trying to see what my nephew was doing in the kitchen. He was not aware that my sister and I were in the room with my nephew - I think it was right after Christmas dinner. My nephew wanted something more to eat because he was not a big fan of Jamaicans' traditional Christmas dinner. He asked if he could have something else. His mother said yes, but when he was about to open the cupboard door he hesitated because he could see Mr. X spying to see what he was taking from the cupboards. I found this to be a little heart-breaking because my nephew did not have the choice in what he wanted to have.

Mr X always showed more of his conniving behaviour when my sister was out of earshot, he used to tell me that my eldest nephew would fail his exams and would not make it anywherebut I had every confidence in my nephew. I felt thatmentally and physically drained from all the complaints and the pettiness of his behaviour. I felt like he was a child and not a grown man. I did not have the confidence to say this to his face because I was living under his roof and I felt uncomfortable about the situation. I even felt very guilty that I had help to steer my sister into this position.

Over the course of time, I sometimes had to play the diplomat between my eldest nephew and him. There is this one particular situation that stands out for me. It made my skin crawl. It was around midday; my nephews, Mr X and I were alone at home. I heard him knocking on my eldest nephew's door accusing him of something. I can't really remember what the accusation was. But I diplomatically said to my nephew try and not do it again. He walked off all smug, thinking that I was on his side, but when he left, I told my nephew, 'next time you are going down call me and I'll go with you.' He agreed to this and I gave him a reassuring smile and went back to my room which was where I spent most of my time now because of his behaviour towards the kids. Two minutes later I heard him calling my name at the bottom of the stairs asking me to come downstairs. I rolled my eyes and went to see him. When I got there he secretly called me in the boy's lounge and gave me a hug which made my skin crawl. In my head, I was thinking that he may possibly have a mental health problem.

By 2017, it had been a rollercoaster ride in the house we had only lived in for three months. He would constantly make jabs at my eldest nephew .He always threatened 'I am going to kick him out of the house for no reason at all'. The only reason I could think of was that my nephew did not cower when he was in a room.

Mr X knew everything about everything. Coming home from work could be an event at times. I dreaded to enter the house and hear what he had to complain about each evening. One evening as soon as I opened the front door Mr X came storming out and calling me to the kitchen to discuss an issue I immediately felt a little depressed and tearful. I didn't know how much more I could take but I could not go to my sister, she was dealing with a lot of stress herself and I did not want to bother her. When I made it to the kitchen he came right out and said that my eldest nephew hit him in the face intentionally. I could not believe this because my nephew was the most peace-loving person I know. I told him this and he elaborated on how this incident happened.

He informed me that when he was showering his son, he placed the shower head over his son's head and proceeded to wash his hair with no warning. My little nephew started to cry and my eldest nephew came rushing out of his room to protect his brother. In the process of arguing he claimed my nephew hit him in the face. But when I got the real version it transpired that my nephe's finger had accidentally touched his the face as he was reaching out to comfort his brother. He went on complaining about this for months.

Somehow Mr X did not seemed to like it when people sat peacefully in a room. He would normally pass through the room about three to four times to get your attention.One day, I needed to use both my fingers and toes to count the number of times he called my sister in one sitting without a break in between. I could see that my sister was getting stressed . My sister got up and went outside for fresh air; he would not even allow that, he had to go out and bother her for something else. I wondered if he was unstable.

When my mother came to stay with us, at first he acted as if everything was okay. I had to roll my eyes every time he did something in goodwill. To impress Mom, Mr X decided to take us on holiday. No one wanted to go but we all felt as if we had to; I can't explain it. Mr. X just booked it and informed us. Luckily no one had anything else planned. My mother started to tell me off for my rude behaviour, however, I told her she would have to wait and see what he was truly like.

Mr. X. tried everything in his power to demotivate my sister. However, he did not succeed because she was the 2017 UK & Ireland Public Speaking champion and a TEDx speaker. He used to make fun about what she does;

saying there is no such thing as a speaking competition. He used to purposely pick fights with my sister for her to lose focus and lose major competitions, but it did not work.

... Mr X along with his relative who was a mental health nurse ruled that my eldest nephew had mental heath problems. He would laugh and repeat that he has mental problems because he had training as a mental health nurse. When my sister heard she cried and kept reassuring Son 1.

During my time in the house of horrors I had become an early riser due to the tension and the coldness of the house. I was normally up around three to four am. I would hear him calling my sister's name repeatedly as she had started to sleep downstairs. He would say something to her but she would not respond. He would keep calling her name until she got up. He would then go back to bed and sleep. This particular scheme would leave my sister tried and in need of sleep. One particular occasion where I found him to be cruel was when he threatened to kick my eldest nephew out of the house because she would not respond to his constant jab session.

In the last couple of days before we left I completely lost respect for Mr X who would antagonize my sister Vinette because she wouldn't always do as he dictated.

That fateful afternoon started off with him coming in from his day of golfing and asking where my sister was. We informed him that she was upstairs resting because she had a headache. He went outside and we all rushed to our rooms. He made his way upstairs and what I could analyse later was that he went upstairs and woke her up. After a while I heard footsteps going downstairs.

We were upstairs for about five to ten minutes when I heard a loud commotion downstairs and my mother and I rushed down - I went ahead of my mother because I could move quicker. When I entered the boys' lounge I found that Mr. X was standing near my sister in an intimidating pose. Her dress was ripped. I felt frightened and unnerved as to what was going on. I felt very angry at this point and wondered if people who have money should have power over everyone else.

My sister grabbed Son 3 and rushed out of the house shouting she was going to the police and he followed. I was so nervous waiting for my sister to get back home. Later, when she got back home, I knew we had to move. I said nothing but I was so happy to be away from Mr X.

Chapter 18
Final Reflections

Today I smiled
Not just from my lips
But from deep within
Today I smiled
At the flowers and the trees
from saplings
weather battered
to majestic avatars
Today I smiled

Today I smiled
At my laughing boys
As they cuddled each other close
and bonds reformed
Today I smiled
As happy memories danced
On sadness juxtaposed
Today I smiled

Today I smiled
As I look at eyes
Filled new-found faith and blissful peace
Today I finally smiled
then closed my eyes and embraced it all
Slowly exhaled and quietly released,
Today I smiled.

Many people may ask, why did I choose to write this book? What do I hope to gain and what impact is it likely to have on my family and friends and indeed my life?

Well before I answer those imaginary questions let me first explain who I am or who I choose to be or, better yet, how I want to be remembered. I never wanted to be remembered as someone who blindly followed traditions or as a person who never asked questions but just accepted the status quo. I am an individual, a unique person, and I never wanted to be a part of the crowd, ever. I have a story, it is my story and I want to tell it. I think many people get so concerned over what others may do or think that they choose never to share their stories and they die with them. I never want that to happen to me. Regarding the impact it may have on others - the truth is, I don't know but this is MY story and just like I have decided to write my story, others may choose to write their own and tell their side; there is no monopoly on book writing. This book is written from my memory and my perspective, it signposts my emotional, psychological and indeed physical journey. It is me.

My initial reason for writing this book was never for publication. I first started writing it as a journal to document my emotions and thoughts and maybe just to keep me sane. It then developed into a therapeutic release from my anger, fears, hopelessness and other negative emotions. Just by writing it down, it felt like it was no longer buried in the recesses on my mind and my emotions slowly regained a sense of balance, although I am not completely there yet. I still have the odd days when the memories and experiences hit me hard, but it has become manageable and now I can smile with authenticity. The same smile that reminded me that tomorrow has the potential to be so much better than today with new possibilities, new chances and new goals. I lived with the belief and knowledge that my life could change with just one simple decision or one random choice and so even in the midst of the pain I was still optimistic about all possible outcomes.

For one entire year, all I could do was write. It became my passion, my obsession, my therapy. I would write between lessons, I would write while cooking or waiting at the traffic lights, in the bathroom, night, day, everywhere and anywhere I would write. Initially I would sit feeling lost and my thoughts would go back and I would remember all the hurt and the pain, the material things I had lost and I would get angry and angrier until my head would start hurting. I would feel as if someone tightened the strings that held my head to my body and I would physically feel pain. So much so that I had to go to the doctor's as I felt I had some unknown disease. The doctor simply put it down to stress and prescribed me Naxofren but that did not help. My pain had passed from the physical and lodged itself in my mind but it felt real and it hurt. In those moments when my pain came I reached for my pen instead of a painkiller and wrote through my pain to make myself better. All my emotions, everything I felt I put it on paper until slowly overtime the pain subsided both physically and emotionally.

My journey has provided me with an opportunity to write. I wrote poems, stories, speeches everything. Sometimes I would only manage one line, other times I would write thousands of words. It's funny because I never considered myself a writer until a fallen angel told me to never write again. I then decided to write and I have not stopped since. In one week I wrote over fifty poems just from my experiences at the time. My mother would remind me that I had no idea where life would take me so to do whatever I was led to do now, to write if I felt like writing, speak of I felt like speaking, walk if I felt like walking. She advised me to be still and just follow my heart.

I try to live my life without regrets but I will always regret what I put my children and family through. I cannot change the past but I will make sure their present and future is filled with happiness and joy.

This book might impact on many people but one of my favourite quotations that I read somewhere and that I live by is: 'The truth may hurt for a little while but a lie will hurt forever.' I would rather be truthful than to pretend and live a lie. I am also mindful of the fact that we are never alone. Anything experienced by one person is usually being experienced somewhere else by someone else. Maybe the names and the places are different but the hurt and pain may be the same. I hope this book will give someone else the strength to speak up and speak out. Maybe my pain and my story may inspire someone somewhere.

My story has helped me to realise that there are people in this world who will utilise their time and focus all their efforts on destroying another human being. It may sound unrealistic and very clinical but one always has to be reminded of the phrase 'what if. . .' and always be prepared for the unexpected. However I never became cynical about love during my whole experience and I fell deeply in love during this most traumatic period of my life which I thought impossible because of my circumstances. I felt my experiences would always be with me. For months I felt unclean. I cannot explain with my vocabulary and even with the assistance of an online thesaurus words just could not convey the emotions, feelings and physical symptoms that I was experiencing. A physical assault is one thing but to be violated mentally and emotionally is a difficult concept to share or convey in words. I thought for many weeks how to express to anyone who may chance to read this journal or book one day. I guess I could relate an experience I had to draw some similarity or parallel to how I felt.

A few years ago we went to a neighbouring park for an afternoon walk. We were comprised of myself, my three boys, Mom and my sister. We spent the day walking, having lunch and just relaxing on blankets we had brought. As I reckoned and closed my eyes I could hear the sound of the leaves rustling as they jostled for the best positions to feel the gently blowing wind. In the background I could hear the laughter of my sons between breathless exhalation as they ran around chasing each other. The occasional shrieks punctuated the laughter as one was caught suddenly then there was the chorus of laughter at the end. I could identify each child and match their laughter without opening my eyes. Funny the things parents can do without thinking, like a super power. I smiled.

As time drifted by we eventually decided it was time to go home. We gathered the left-over morsels of biscuits and wrappers, discarded shoes and jumpers, blankets and one sleepy child and headed to our cars.

There was a slight odour as we walked to the car but no one spoke about it; probably each assuming it was a gaseous escape by one of the other parties. We continued talking nonchalantly about any and every random thing, conversations merging into each other seamlessly. The smell persisted. I assumed we must be walking past some rotting organic matter or discarded excrement and anticipated relief or fresh air after a few more steps but still the smell persisted.

Just as I started wondering if everyone was smelling what I was also smelling my sister asked, 'Who is that man? Someone needs the toilet?' she questioned pulling the neck of her jumper up to cover her nose.

'It is Son 1,' Son 2 shouted.

'No it is not,' Son 1 retorted reaching out to slap the head of his brother who moved briskly out of his reach resulting in his arms flailing through the air and unintentionally slapping his own thighs after losing the initial momentum. Son 2 giggled. Son3 just looked a bit exhausted and merely raised his head from the shoulders of my sister who had been carrying him in her arms. Uninterested he stuck his thumb in his mouth and went back to dozing on her shoulder.

The momentary distractions was not enough to eradicate the smell. Suspicious and accusatory glances were being cast around the group by everyone. 'Someone ate something that was spoilt man!' Son 2 echoed and we laughed, but cautiously not opening our mouths too much for the smell to enter through the open orifice.

The smell followed us to the car. I got into it with my sons, and my sister and Mom got into the other car. I started the engine and dheadedtowards home. The smell was still there. I was just about to speak when the phone rang and Son 1 answered, 'yes Gramma !' There was a pause for the other side to speak then his response, 'no, it is still here ! We can still smell it!' He turned away from the phone and directed his conversation towards me. 'Grandma says it must be one of us because she can't smell it anymore,' and then with a lowered tone he whispered conspiratorially, ' I think it is Son 3. He's the only one who hasn't denied it,' then snickered.

I furrowed my brows and cast him an annoyed glance.

' I think we should wake Son 3 and check,' Son 2 declared.

'Can you all stop?' I shouted through clenched teeth somehow thinking the odour wouldn't get in. I cracked open the windows to get fresh air.

'Bye grandma !' Son 3 whispered into the phone, 'see you soon,' then quickly added, 'if we make it,' then hung up.

No response from me, half through frustration and the other half was this nauseating sickly, itches-your-throat smell. When I could not take it any longer I pulled over and tapped onto my inner sniffer dog trying to pinpoint the source of the offending smell. After a few minutes we found it,

I stood next to Son 1 and Son 2 staring at Son 3. We must have presented a comical picture for anyone passing by. Son 3 shifted and groggily opened his eyes and realised he was alone and lying on the back seat of my mom's car. The door was opened and he could see us standing there faces screwed up and just staring at him. Curiosity gave way to alarm and then panic. Son 3 sat up abruptly: 'Mom?'

I grimaced then took s step closer. 'Hon did you poo your pants?'

Overwhelmed and comprehending the situation he started to cry. I reached out and cuddled him then pulled at the waist of his trousers to check if he had any organic deposits. Nothing. Puzzled, I sat him on the backseat and went back into sniffer dog mode. Then I found it stuck to the bottom of Son 3's shoe - a dark gooey lump mixed with grass and pebbles and reeking. I held my breath and slowly and carefully removed the offending article of clothing. The first thought was to throw the shoes away but having just bought them for £30 I decided that a good wash would remedy the situation. I picked up a broken twig and attempted to dislodge most of the foreign material but bits still clung in the groove of the shoe. The shoes were tied in a plastic bag found in the boot of my car and locked in the trunk but still the smell persisted on the drive home = but somehow more manageable once we knew the cause of the rancid odour.

We eventually made it home and the first item in the

agenda was to get that shoe in the wash. I took the bag from the boot at arm's length and walked to the back of my house, turned on the tap outside and let it run over the sole of the shoe to remove even more of the organic matter, then placed it inside the washing machine added soap and freshener and turned it on.

Weeks after the incident, despite several clean-outs and air freshener it seemed the smell was still there so strong you could almost taste it at the back of your throat. The smell was just there. Whether it was mind over matter is irrelevant. I just could not get rid of that smell.

My emotional state had many similarities. Even though I had walked away from Mr X, like a bad smell his presence lingered with me and would not go. During the days when I kept busy all would be well because I was temporarily distracted but as soon as the noise stopped and the quiet of night descended, once again he was there like a dark foreboding shadow. I couldn't shake it and I felt stifled and scared. Then there was the insomnia. I could not sleep for more than two hours. I would count sheep, drink milk but to no avail. Eventually to get some peace, I would get up and write.

Life is all about balance and no one is ever completely down and out; there is always a positive or some slither of hope, one just have to search for it but it is always there. Hold on to that and life will guide you through that darkest tunnel into the light. Love is by far the most powerful force in the universe. The right type of love can lift you from the depths of despair and let you soar like an eagle. There are certain types of love that will always be there, like the love of a mother or of siblings or the love of children. They are very important in giving you a foundation and a never-ending source of balance but sometimes as human beings we take them for granted and forget their importance when the dark times come. Refresh and replenish these loves frequently and strengthen them before you need them.

The love of God transcends everything that you can fathom. It fills you completely and gives you a certain calm and peace that is indescribable to someone unless they experience it for themselves. For me it was like walking amongst lions, bears tigers snakes and feeling no fear, just a surreal serenity and calmness that gave the assurance that all is well and it cannot be any other way. I know that I had already won before the race had ended; it was that faith in the process. Although I wavered occasionally whenever I reached for spiritual guidance I felt his presence. For those who believe, time is always the deal breaker in any bargain between the spiritual realm and our perceived reality, patience the mediator. Learn to wait!

Then there is the love shared between a man and a woman. a love that has no boundaries nor conditions, a love that is beyond the physical. I knew my life partner was the one before any form of physical contact. We didn't need to touch, there was a chemistry and connection that I had never experienced before. His voice would calm me and my problems would disappear for that moment. Everything in life happens for a reason whether we realise it or not, in beautiful 'synchronicity'. A simple act, response or reaction may change your life without you ever knowing.

I think I have become so obsessed with the vibrations of the universe and the interconnectedness of everything that I now constantly focus on the 'why' instead of 'what, where, when, who and how'! I read about two books each month just to get a better understanding and to discover the perspective of others who wanted to know too. I have spent many hours in silence and in the dark of my room listening for some answers. I did not rule out any possibility. It could have come from the physical world, the dream world or signs, I did not know but listened and sometimes I heard. I am not sure if I only heard my answers because I desperately wanted to hear them or I heard them simply because I was listening. Whatever the reason, I heard them. I remember reading a book The Alchemist and Santiago mentioned that butterflies were omens of good luck. I paused and thought to myself, 'well I am certainly not going to see any butterflies' as it was winter. Sure enough my birthday was the next day and my sons gave me a card with exactly forty-one butterflies. Coincidence??? Maybe but I doubt it. I will keep that card forever.

Sometimes my signs appeared as fallen angels that created obstacles, but overcoming these obstacles made me stronger and pushed me to higher heights.

I learnt to listen. Not just to what was being said but everything and took the message. Once I became open to listening I was amazed at how many messages came my way. I was once wandering around in Sainsbury's trying to find a Jamaican food item. I stood in the middle of the aisle scanning the shelves, moving my head from side to side quickly when an elderly gentleman approached me. Our eyes met and he smiled and said 'You look like you're searching for something, you'll find it quicker if you ask' and carried on shopping. I stood there for a while repeating what he had said in my head. On any other ordinary day I would have just smiled and would not give another thought to it. But that day, on that very morning, I was stuck in what my next steps in life should be. The elderly man had reminded me that I can ask for help sometimes. I smiled and wrote the sentence in my little notepad right in the middle of the supermarket aisle.

I learned to ask. I asked my mom and family when I needed help, which is an important thing to learn. However I also found that sometimes you may not get the help that you request. If however you trust the process sometimes the wrong answers may lead you indirectly to the right place but you've got to have faith.

*****

I have no doubts that I will become a regular fixture in the British court system because of Mr X as he utilises this method with the sole intention of draining me financially; I have been repeatedly threatened with this. If I am one minute late I expect a solicitor's letter at my door, if I say something it is another solicitor letter and even when I choose to remain silent I'll get one for lack of communication. Mr X has always maintained that I have made false allegations against him and he was scared to come near me. Yet later when I applied for a non-molestation order his solicitors wrote to say it was unjustified. . I applied after Mr X posted his friend to stand outside my front door for forty five minutes under the pretence that he was there to collect his son. It always puzzled me why he still wanted the freedom to be outside my home. Common sense would dictate that he would choose stay as far away from me as possible.

If I should ask you who was the sixth woman you saw on your way to work this morning chances are you would not remember because it was not important to you and so your brain has dismissed this fact as irrelevant. Through pain and dedicated effort and time I have done the same to Mr X.

My family have grown closer. My children especially have developed a protective relationship towards me. It is not infrequent for them to hug me and I frequently shout 'I love you' in the middle of any and everything. I hold on to these things dearly because in time they may fade and lessen. I have however, due to the transitory nature of life, ensured that they find something inside to hold on to and not me as a physical person. I have taught them the value of relationships and how to be strong but reminded them that, as mere human beings, we are not permanent. Treasure each moment but be strong from inside so you can be resilient in the storms of life. Be like the bamboo and bend gracefully then rebound when the time is right.

They have learnt that material things are but for a while. Value them but do not become too attached. Treasure memories deep inside that can never be erased. My sons always remember that your circumstances are not you and life can change in the blink of an eye. Finally make your decision your own and do not be easily swayed by others.

My financial situation had taken a hit that will take time to recover from but I am ready. I am stronger and my mindset is more focussed towards this achievement, if not for myself then for my children, my mother and my sister who have stood side by side on the frontline with me. Our bonds have been forged together by pain and struggles and have become unbreakable.

My job I mourned but for a millisecond. If the truth be told, I was not happy there but like so many millions of us we think of the bills and all the what-ifs instead of chasing our dreams with passion and zeal and we wake up one morning only to find life has past us by. Do I hate anyone in this process? Absolutely not! Every person in your life must fulfil their role, positive or negative so allow them to be who they were created to be. I am sure I have wronged people too and done things to cause offence in my past. Why should I be so self-righteous in thinking that everyone else is wrong but I am always right? Most times it is not even about who is wrong or who is right; it is all about perspective. I always try to rise above the situation and try to get the bird's-eye view. As I flew to Texas recently and looked outside my plane window I didn't even see my workplace, such was its insignificance in the grand scheme of things. Its magnitude lies only in my mind and in the space I allow it to take up in my mind. Today it occupies a minuscule reference file that I can use for future choices and decisions.

My love life is still a work in progress but I believe I have found my soulmate - which may not translate into being my physical partner for the future but I will always have this love inside of me for all eternity. It is a love of a person, not what they look like, what they have, where they live or what they take to the table. It is a deep spiritual connection that I am glad I was able to experience in my lifetime. We will see where it goes but I am not anxious or fearful; I am calm and serene and willing to flow with the universe.

So where am I now in my journey?

I am at peace.

I have accepted what I cannot change. I am not responsible for anyone else's actions; I can only control my reactions and actions. I bear no ill will or malice to anyone and I am certain everything will work out, maybe not the way I want but the way it is supposed to. I accept life's challenges each day with a smile and a gratitude that I still have my faith, family and wonderful friends.

Am I strong?

Sometimes I get so tired of acting strong
Trying to figure out exactly where I belong
Playing to the same old song
Following the unthinking throng
Acting right but feeling wrong
Quietly being dragged along

I am weary of pretending to be
Exactly what you think of me
Look deep inside and see
My hidden reality
Yearning and longing to be free
I simply just want to be me !

I decide. . . .

Today as I reflect on the past year
With all its joys and the inevitable tears
I can clearly see the lessons I have learnt
And remember all the places where I got badly burnt
I'll focus with joy on my fondest memories
And put them all together under the title '2017 summaries'

Looking forward to 2018 and all the potential it brings
When all around the world, the new year ring
I shall make no resolutions
No absolutions
No new constitutions
Or stirred up revolutions

Instead this year I will add one phrase
That will herald in my newest phase
The words I will use are simple 'I decide'
In 2018 this will be my only guide
I'll decide where to go and who to see
And just who'll be in my closest company
I'll decide which path to pursue
It will all be up to me and not to you
I will choose my destiny
Create my own identity
I'll decide who and how to love
Will focus less on people but look above
I will decide what, where, when and why
Because my life's purpose will be forged by only 'I'

I will decide!

Behind this smile – my sons

My three sons I will love you to the very end
On that you can forever depend
I know that I have made a few mistakes
thinking the end goal was for your sake
I thought I was creating a happy home
A settled place so we would no more roam
But paradise quickly changed to hell
And a saving angel changed to an infidel
With no visible options to choose
I had to stay and endure the abuse
I tried to protect you the best I can
And quickly had to develop a new game plan
I know you were all affected
And this is something that will always be regretted
Never again will I put you boys in this position
This is my sincere and genuine proposition

I wrote a few more lines then slowly I fell asleep.
Good night.

About the Author

Vinette is a speaker, trainer and writer. She is the author of Did the Right Sperm Win? Books 1&2 and Vinette's Vignettes. She was born in St Thomas, Jamaica but migrated to the UK in 2002.

She is an avid reader and enjoy nature walks, classic cars and public speaking.

Her recent personal experiences have made her enrol to study for a degree in Psychology so she can better understand the motivation of others.

Vinette is a Christian and mother of three phenomenal boys. She would like to be remembered as a kind and considerate person. Her life's quest is for spiritual enlightenment and awakening.

22174470R00128

Printed in Great Britain
by Amazon